Dina El Shammaa is a seasoned author whose extensive writing background helps her uncover unexpected daily occurrences that affect the lives of millions of women in the region and beyond in her novel 'The Trials of Allura'.

Being a full-time hard-working mother of two does not stop Dina from continuing to write stories based on true events, regardless of what the genre may be.

She follows her intuition, born of a realistic understanding of day-to-day circumstances surrounding the ordinary human being, without any type of fluff or exaggeration, which is why her next work is even more factual.

Dina's respected readers admire the honesty and simplicity in her writing, which is why she persists in conveying realistic messages, with hopes of creating a lasting legacy of ethical writing.

This book is dedicated to my two beautiful angels, who give me strength and inspire me each and every single day.

From the moment you were born, I knew my life would change. You've given me all the courage I needed to write this book. I have to thank you for that:

Mia and Adam

I am grateful you are in my world. I hope that one day I will make you both proud. I love you both, with all my heart and till my last breath.

Dina El Shammaa

THE TRIALS OF ALLURA

AUSTIN MACAULEY PUBLISHERS™
LONDON • CAMBRIDGE • NEW YORK • SHARJAH

ISBN – 9789948253266 – (Paperback)
ISBN – 9789948253259 – (E-Book)

Application Number: MC-10-01-3155402
Age Classification: 17+

Printer Name: iPrint Global Ltd
Printer Address: Witchford, England

First Published (2021)
AUSTIN MACAULEY PUBLISHERS FZE
Sharjah Publishing City
P.O Box [519201]
Sharjah, UAE
www.austinmacauley.ae
+971 655 95 202

I want to thank the special people in my life who have always believed in me, encouraged me and boosted my confidence, and to those who have stood by me while writing this book, whether personally or professionally. I am forever grateful. Your support will always be appreciated and never forgotten.

I would particularly like to thank my parents, Ms Ninette El Shammaa and Dr. Essam El Shammaa, who sacrificed a lot just to ensure I received the right type of education and upbringing.

Mum and Dad, thank you for helping me achieve my dream. It was you who discovered the writer within me at a very young age, and continue to encourage me to pursue what I love the most.

You have always been a source of strength and support, and without you I would not have been who I am today. Thank you for your ongoing reinforcement, patience and for believing in me all those years.

Preface

It wasn't an easy decision to write this book. It needed a lot of inspiration, motivation, free time, multi-tasking and determination, especially with two young children and a full-time job.

I've been meaning to write a book for more than 20 years, but I wasn't in what they call 'the writer's inspirational state of mind'. Deciding to write a novel, especially one that is real and inspired by true events, is a huge responsibility. It requires an enormous amount of imagination and inspiration. But when the time was right, I seized the opportunity to get started. Any person who considers themselves a talented writer will probably relate to that.

My first attempt to write anything was when I was six years old. I was curious to see what I could create with a pen and paper. The results were exciting, surprising and memorable. I ended up writing my first personalised poem, which was actually published by a reputable English daily newspaper. Family and friends were supportive at the time, recognising my talent and passion for writing, which I've worked hard to hone over the years.

My passion for writing encouraged me to study Media and Journalism at university. Strangely though, I ended up working in a lot of jobs that did not involve writing, because I was curious about trying different professions and wanted to experiment and figure out what I was good at. Eventually, I found myself yearning to write again and went back to media relations and writing. I truly believe that when you're passionate about what you do, you thrive faster than you'd ever expect, so while I was anxious about starting a completely new career in the media field, I excelled faster than I expected; I jumped from being a Junior Writer to a Senior Reporter, Chief Reporter and then a Deputy Editor, which is when I left for a media related position in a reputable government entity.

I thoroughly enjoyed writing *The Trials of Allura*. I could see the incidents happening clearly in my mind, as though I was watching the events unfold in a movie. What helped me while writing this novel was that the incidents are all real. Everything that Allura has gone through happened to women I personally know, or know of.

I aspire that many women, whether from the Middle East or elsewhere, will relate to Allura's character and the type of adverse incidents she had to experience.

It is unfortunate that plenty of educated Middle Eastern women still face some of the challenges that Allura went through, yet decide to remain silent about their situation. What's even more despairing is that those particular women are the ones who are mostly misunderstood, sometimes by the people closest to them, and definitely by the outside world, who wrongly perceive them as vulnerable and spoilt. Quite the opposite, it is those exact women who are the toughest. They stand tall in times of despair and are indomitable during the roughest moments. They thrive to remain optimistic despite the different challenges they endure in life.

This compelling emotional story mimics some of the hardships women go through. As an example, despite the cultural constraints forced on a Middle Eastern woman to get married by a particular age, many choose to remain single and work hard to make ends meet. Those women are great at what they do and have fruitful career paths, yet are still underpaid and underappreciated in comparison to their male counterparts.

Others are single mothers and/or breadwinners who are expected to multi-task and keep up with life's busy pace; they keep up with a demanding job, children, family obligations and cultural expectations, resulting in little or no break at all, and are not given as little as a 'pat on the shoulder'.

Several women experience abuse, whether mentally, emotionally or physically. They are forced to tolerate how their partners/husbands treat them for the sake of their children, or in fear that society would be unkind to them.

The Trials of Allura is a testament to the talents and resilience of extraordinary women that echoes some of the difficulties and obligations women are forced to be a part of. This tempestuous character chose to rail against life's challenges. It isn't easy for Allura to move away from everything she had ever known, then be forced to become a part of a society she knows nothing about, despite her family heritage.

Readers may be shocked to hear that women in this part of the world go through many challenges of their own, if not worse. Bottom line is: 'We are all more similar than one might expect.'

It's important to consider a woman's voice in the Middle East, and to reflect on some of the things she's required to become a part of without her consent.

I truly hope you enjoy reading The Trials of Allura, as much as I enjoyed writing it.

Blessings, peace and love.

Dina El Shammaa

Prologue

Allura sat frozen in shock. Her body felt sore, and when she shifted slightly, a sharp pain rose from below her waist.

Throwing back the covers, she nearly let out a wail. She had no recollection of how she had ended up naked and alone in a bed. Panicking, Allura frantically began to look for her clothes and personal belongings, but they were nowhere to be found.

Spying a discarded mobile phone on the side table, she switched it on and let out a sigh of relief when it turned out to be unlocked. Allura tried to remember Moe's number, since he was the last person she recalled spending time with at the party, but her trembling hands punched in the first number that came to mind. Raising the phone to her ear, she anxiously counted each ring until her former boss and confidant picked up the line.

Ahmed, luckily, answered right away. Allura was shaking with fear.

"Dr Ahmed! Dr Ahmed, it's me, Allura. P—please help me. I'm in danger." Allura sobbed, feebly attempting to whisper in the darkened room.

Once he started to reply, she felt reassured and couldn't care less about how loud her voice was. The music was loud enough, and it occurred to her that things couldn't get worse than they already were.

"Allura? What's going on? Where are you now? Whose number is this?" Ahmed asked anxiously, his lips curled back from his teeth in a half-snarl as he dashed about his room looking for something to wear.

She then noticed that her thighs were covered with blood. She burst into tears, her body in spasms under her heavy sobs.

Her voice was shaky and broken in terror, and Ahmed's heart froze at the sound of it. "I was…I…" was all she managed to spit out. Her words were shattered by fear and shock. "I'm at a—a party, and…" She broke down in frantic sobbing. "I don't know what to do! Please…I was…raped!" She struggled to breathe, to think, to speak. "Help me. Help me, please!"

"OK, listen to me, Allura, and try to answer briefly. I know you can hardly talk right now. What are you noticing around you, are there any landmarks or things that would give you an idea where you are?"

"I can't focus. I can't think!" she wailed, tugging her hair frantically.

"Yes, you can. Now get a hold of yourself. You must calm down and get out of there in one piece. Now!"

Ahmed took a few breaths and decided to calm himself down too, realising that losing his temper would bring nothing but more harm.

"OK, listen. Let's both calm down. Let's both take deep breaths together. Exhale and inhale. And please, Allura, stay focused on what I'm about to ask you. Now once again, where exactly are you right now?"

It took a few deep breaths and tremendous effort to block the thought of being raped from her mind before she could answer.

"I—I'm in a bedroom, at a beach house. I don't know…it's in Ain Al Sokhna somewhere." Rivulets of tears continued to run uncontrollably down her cheeks. Her heart was pounding, her body was shaking and her legs felt numb.

"Do you see any windows or a way out of the room you're in right now, some sort of exit?" he asked as he slid the key in the ignition.

She looked around and spotted a balcony that led to the front yard garden and nodded distractedly. "Yes, yes! I see a balcony. What do I do now?"

"Walk towards the balcony and describe what you see."

From the window, she spotted a nearby hotel in the area that Ahmed was familiar with. She explained that she could reach that hotel if he stayed with her on the line for emotional support.

Allura wiped a hand across her tearstained face, smudging an abundant amount of makeup in the process. She tried to concentrate on what Ahmed was saying and decided to get herself together.

"OK, now, look for any suitable clothes around, and put them on. Is there a cupboard in the room you're in?"

"Yes, there's a cupboard here."

"Open it. Grab anything appropriate and put it on," suggested Ahmed. He was already in his car driving towards where she was located.

Meanwhile, Allura decided to fight the feeling of numbness and tingling across her hands, feet, arms and legs and forced herself to move a bit faster.

"My body really hurts," she complained tearfully, feeling sorry for herself.

"You're doing well. You need to be brave. Once you're fully dressed, let me know."

Allura hesitated. Taking a deep breath, she finally opened the cupboard hastily, grabbed the first shirt and sweatpants she saw, and slipped her feet into a convenient pair of flip-flops.

She gasped for air as she stood in front of the cupboard for a few seconds, relieved that she had some clothes on her again.

"I'm dressed. Now what? I'm completely lost. Please don't leave me, Ahmed, please."

"I need you to remain calm and focused. This is the hardest part now. Only listen to my voice, OK, Allura?"

"I'll try. Just stay with me. I need you with me. Don't hang up, OK?"

"I'm here, Allura. I'm not going anywhere. Just listen carefully. Go back to the balcony, and tell me where it leads to exactly? Is it on the top or bottom floor?"

Allura took painful steps towards the veranda, which overlooked the front entrance of the house.

She peered in through the glass window as it slid open. The spacious veranda was at street level. The coast was clear.

"It's on the bottom floor. All the noise is coming from the backyard by the beach and pool area. I can still hear the crazy crowd partying. I can see an exit to the street outside! What do I do now?" she mumbled anxiously.

"Look around you again. Is there anyone in sight?"

"No, I can't see anyone at all."

"OK, you're doing really well so far. I need you to calmly and slowly exit the house now, OK?"

"I can't! He'll see me! He'll hurt me again!"

"Allura, I promise, whoever this punk is, he won't hurt you again. Now, you need to stay strong, OK? Take one step at a time, start with the balcony and move ahead from there. I'm right here, I promise." Ahmed's body was trembling in rage. Taking a deep breath, he focused on Allura's soft breaths for a few seconds.

"I'm at the veranda outside now; I'm going to run as fast as I can, OK?"

"Perfect, spot on! Now keep the phone on. Just place it in your pocket or anywhere safe and run towards the exit. Get the hell out of there as fast as you can. Head towards the nearby hotel we spoke about. Don't say anything or attempt to speak to anyone in the meantime. I want you to focus on one thing and only one thing: getting there! The second you reach the hotel, put the phone back to your ear. If it disconnects, I'll phone you back, and I'll be at the lobby in less than two hours!"

Despite the excruciating pain, Allura limped as fast as she could towards the hotel, praying she'd make it in one piece without being harmed even further.

How could have everything gone so wrong in just one year?

One Year Ago

Chapter 1

Allura's Big Surprise

It was right after Haitham gifted Sawsan with the perfume called Allure that the idea came to mind. They were in Paris when their life-changing news arrived. The perfume was to celebrate their discovery that Sawsan was pregnant with a baby girl.

"Why don't we call her Allura? Let's look at what the name means!"

They learned that Allura meant 'to entice or attract'. Even better, the name was originally French, so the decision to name her Allura was made even easier by the fact that they received the wonderful news whilst they were in Paris, the city of romance.

Their minds were made up. What better name could they have picked out for their miracle child? Allura it was! She was a product of love, the result of years of attempts, tears, frustrations and constant hope to conceive a child.

Even though she was an only child who was doted on and spoiled by her parents, Allura was raised with the strict values of a good and moral person. As she grew up, Sawsan and Haitham made sure to teach her about her roots, telling her about life in Egypt and Lebanon.

Allura was always encouraged to engage in sports, particularly swimming. She had a promising future, taking part in many competitions, including a regional one for swimmers under sixteen. There she won first prize and established a new speed record in the butterfly category. While it was something she was passionate about, Allura wasn't sure swimming was something she wanted to dedicate her life to, despite constant encouragement from her coach and parents.

She was also popular at school, and had a large group of friends. A brunette, Allura was five-foot-seven, with beautiful wide blue eyes, shoulder-length black hair, and tanned skin. As a result, she had been offered modelling work on various occasions, but she always felt too shy to take it up. Her enticing personality was complex: she was timid yet brave, fragile yet strong, outspoken, and at times impulsive, but also intensely private.

Allura attended a private British school and had plenty of friends from various countries. She loved the diversity of her school and always looked forward to befriending people from different parts of the world. Her multicultural background confused her even more when her parents decided to change countries and move from Abu Dhabi in the United Arab Emirates to Cairo, the capital of Egypt.

"Allura, I need to speak with you. Do you have a few minutes?" asked Sawsan.

"What is it, Mum? I'm all sweaty." She had just returned from swim practice at school.

"This won't take much time. Sweetheart, your father has been asked to leave his company. It's nothing personal, and he did nothing wrong. His contract just ended, and as much as we'd love to keep living in this beautiful country, we have to go back to Egypt."

Haitham had been working in an oil company in Abu Dhabi for fourteen years. When he first received the offer, the couple considered it a great opportunity to raise their child in a multi-ethnic yet Arab society, where their daughter could learn about and value different cultures while still maintaining a connection to her own roots.

Allura had been only two when the family left London to move to Abu Dhabi. Haitham was a talented engineer, but he worked with the company on a contractual basis; that was part of the original agreement. He had initially agreed to move to Abu Dhabi for two years, but his contract kept getting renewed due to his outstanding contributions. However, when he turned sixty, the company was forced to let him go.

"Egypt?" Allura said, the despair in her soul obvious in her tone. "I know nothing about that place. What on earth are we going to do in Egypt? All my friends are here. Mum, this is horrible news!"

"I know. I'm sorry I had to break the news to you this way, but there's just no other way. You're sixteen now, Allura. You're old enough to understand things."

Allura felt confused. What was she going to do in Egypt, a country she barely knew anything about? Her roots were Egyptian, but she had lived all her life in the UAE; she knew nothing else. Her parents had always meant to take Allura to Egypt during her summer holidays but, despite their best intentions, the family always ended up travelling around Europe or the UK.

She was shattered and thought about all the friends she'd leave behind – and the country that she had fallen in love with and considered her own.

"But I have two more years to go before I enter university! Mum, I can't go back to Egypt now. Why can't I stay here until I finish school? Maybe we can ask someone to sponsor me or something."

Allura was one of the brightest pupils in her grade and had already made plans to study abroad.

"Allura, that's absolutely out of the question. You are going to Egypt with us, and that's final. We're leaving next month, so I need you to start packing all your things and leave behind the unnecessary items."

"Next month?" she grumbled as various thoughts of future losses crossed her mind: the school mate she had a crush on and was about to date, the close friends she had known since kindergarten and her professional swimming classes. The initial idea of having to leave for university after high school had been daunting enough, and now she had to deal with this.

"Are you sure there's no way I can stay behind? Consider it a trial separation for when I go to university?" Allura tried to joke.

Her mother frowned. "This isn't funny. Please take this seriously. Your dad needs both our support. The move is not easy on him, either. Do you think either your dad or I saw this coming? We knew he was approaching retirement, but had no idea he'd be asked to leave before he turned 65. Having to force you to leave school in the beginning of your school year like this isn't exactly the ideal situation for any of us, I realise that, but at times we need to accept things as they are!"

Allura grew angry. "How am I supposed to support Dad when you've both decided to ruin my life without telling me? I thought we were a family that decided everything together. Guess I was wrong!" she screamed before stomping to her bedroom and slamming the door.

Lying on the bed, Allura fought back tears as she thought about how her life was about to change forever.

The next day, Allura broke the news to her friends at school. Everyone was disappointed to hear she was leaving, but they were determined to cheer her up. They decided to throw a farewell party in her honour, and this helped to lift her spirits temporarily.

For the next few days, Allura and her friends were working on the invitee list for the farewell party. That got Allura busy. Being positive by nature, she started to divert her thoughts to the more exciting idea.

That day, Sawsan picked Allura up from school. The Mahmoud family owned two cars, a Jeep that her mother drove, and a two-seater sports car that Haitham treated as his own baby.

"How was your day, darling?" Sawsan asked as Allura settled down in the passenger seat.

"Super, Mum! I had to tell all my friends at school that I'm suddenly leaving. How do you think it went?"

"Allura, I know this is hard, but think of the bright side. Think of the new friends you'll be making once you move to Egypt. You'll have a brand-new life with new beginnings. It's exciting and fun. Besides, you have family over there!"

"I have family there? How come you never mentioned that before?"

"It's complicated, darling. You know that my family all live in Lebanon. As for your father's family…well, they are scattered. They live in different areas in Egypt, and we unfortunately lost touch with them a long time ago. However, it's an excellent opportunity for us to reconnect and for you to meet them once we move there."

"But why didn't you ever mention them before? I thought Dad was an orphan or something! Are there any more surprises I should know about? Like, are we royalty? Are you and Dad in some sort of witness-protection programme?"

"Allura, stop being so rude! I understand you're frustrated right now, and you have every reason to be. Your father and I should have told you about a lot of things a long time ago. We've always tried our best to do what we felt was best for you, but that doesn't necessarily mean we were right about our decisions all the time. We're human; we are bound to make mistakes."

"Yeah, like keeping me in the dark about a whole family I have back in Egypt! Mum, I don't want to have this conversation anymore; I'm really sick of it. By the way, you never mentioned which school I'm going to or where we'll be living in Egypt. Did you know Egypt has a population of a hundred million? How on earth am I going to fit in there?"

Sawsan sighed. She parked in their designated spot and turned to her distressed daughter. "Sweetie, everything will be just fine. I love you, and so does your father. Everything will work out. Speaking of which, I got you a little something."

Allura opened the envelope and gasped at the money it contained. "What am I supposed to do with all of this, Mum?"

"Well, whatever you want," Sawsan replied, caressing her daughter's face. "How about buying some new clothes and accessories? I'm sure you'd like to get together with your friends a few times before we move, so why not go out with a bang?"

Allura looked apprehensive as she held the money in her hand. She had no idea what her mum had in mind but knew that she was trying all she could to make her feel better, as always.

As they walked towards the elevators, Sawsan drew Allura in for a hug, causing the young woman to tear up.

"I'm sorry, Mum. I don't mean to be a brat. I'm just freaking out. I'm suddenly told that my life is about to change in less than a month, with new friends, a new family and a new country. It's just too much to take on."

"I know, love, and I completely understand. I just want you to know how much we love you and will always look after you, regardless of where it is we end up," said Sawsan as she hugged Allura tight. "Just trust that everything will be OK."

On most days, Sawsan had the perfect relationship with her daughter. She listened to her, spoke with her, spent quality time with her and was patient. Haitham, on the other hand, always looked out for his baby girl and at times was considered too protective by Allura, her mum and the people that knew them the most.

Allura viewed Sawsan as a strong, accomplished woman who gave everything its due diligence, from working her way up until she was awarded for her top-notch research findings in the field of education, to giving up on a prosperous future just to take care of her daughter. Allura found it intriguing how Sawsan prioritised things with such passion while making her exertions look effortless. She was very proud of her mother and considered her selfless and tremendously intelligent.

Time quickly flew by, and suddenly it was the week of her farewell party. Allura regarded the event with mixed emotions. On one hand, her friends and, more importantly, her crush, James, were going to be there. On the other hand, it would be the end of the only life she had ever known.

A day before the beach party, which was going to take place at one of the famous hotels in the capital, Allura and her friends went shopping with the aim of buying her a head-turning dress that would capture James's attention.

Trying on a monochrome, geometric-print black and white dress, Allura contemplated buying it.

"Allura Mahmoud! If you're thinking what I think you're thinking, I'm going to take your money away! Don't you dare buy that dress! Especially since it'll be the first time in history that you wear one!" hooted Maria Quiros, one of Allura's best friends.

"What's wrong with it?" Allura asked quizzically.

"It's the type of dress my grandmother wouldn't even choose to wear. What's wrong with you? You're only sixteen! Besides, you're tall. You have beautifully shaped legs and a killer body. Show it off, girl! Trust me, James will appreciate the effort," her other friend, Rola Aboud, said with a mischievous wink.

The final friend in the group, Helen Brant, dragged Allura around the shop until she stopped before a particular dress on a mannequin. "This is it. Try this on!"

"This is what?" asked Allura with a sneaky smile on her face.

"This is the dress you're trying on, you nitwit!"

The rest of the girls gathered around Allura and shouted in agreement. "Perfect, that's more like it!"

The ruby-red, above-the-knee, flared chiffon spaghetti-strapped dress was accentuated by a plunging V-neckline, supportive boning and flattering seam lines, and assisted by a flirtatious-looking swingy skirt.

"Are you all crazy? I can't possibly wear this. My father would kill me!" Allura said.

"Haitham is like the coolest father ever. You're just coming up with excuses because you're too chicken to wear something different. This dress is pure elegance, it'll look ravishing on you! Try it on. Don't be fast to judge," suggested Rola.

"Fine, I'll try it on. But I tell you, this is too daring. I can't possibly leave the house looking like this."

"Looking like what? The dress is young and fresh. There's nothing indecent about it. Besides, we'll be at the beach. It's not like you can wear a long-sleeved, conservative loose gown. Well, you could, but we wouldn't let you," said Helen impatiently.

Allura was pretty open-minded, yet she had some conservative views about certain things. She took the best traits from the worlds of both east and west. She was reserved yet honest. She had been taught how to respect different beliefs but not back down from her own convictions.

While trying on the dress, Allura turned to look at herself in the mirror and, to her surprise, loved what she saw.

"Wow!" she said to herself. She felt and looked like a grown-up lady in the glamorous dress. She loosened her hair around her shoulders as she twirled on her tiptoes in the dressing room.

As she walked out, her friends were speechless.

"Wow, wow, weezers! Look at you!" said Maria with a huge grin. "You've transformed, woman!"

On most days, Allura wore either a simple shirt and trousers or her school uniform. She had hardly been seen in a dress before.

"James is so going to dig this," said Maria, laughing.

"I'm absolutely stunned. You look outstanding, Allura. You have to buy this dress!" urged Helen.

"Well, I don't know. I feel fabulous, but it's so not me. I don't—"

Before she could continue her sentence, her friends dragged her to the counter, where Allura was forced to buy the dress as well as the complementary sandals they had picked out for her.

Purchase in hand, she thought about the remaining money in her purse. Biting her lip, Allura looked around. She could spend it on additional accessories or clothes, but a glittering pendant caught her attention. Allura felt a bit guilty at the way she had been treating her parents, and thought it would be nice to get them a couple of gifts to show her appreciation. Exiting the store, Allura felt lighter as she and her friends continued enjoying their day out.

That night, Allura was so excited that she just had to show her parents her new dress. Haitham was sitting on the living room couch surfing the Internet while Sawsan sat nearby, reading a book.

"Mum, Dad. I have something to show you, but please promise you won't overreact."

"What is it, honey?" asked Sawsan, smiling.

"Well, I brought a dress today for my farewell party. I'd really like to show it to you, but I'm worried you won't approve," she said.

Haitham looked up. She had suddenly caught his attention. "And why is it that we wouldn't like the dress, Allura?"

"See, Daddy? I knew it. You're judging the dress before even seeing it on me. I can't believe you!"

"Allura! I am not judging anything. I'm simply responding to what you've just said. Show us the dress. Now, you've got me curious."

She calmed down. "OK, Daddy, but promise me you won't get upset. I really love this dress!"

"Fine, Allura. We're waiting. Put it on."

Sawsan smiled as Allura ran out of the room. "Our baby has grown, Haitham. She's actually wearing a dress now. Do you know how many times I tried to convince her to wear anything halfway feminine? I still remember her tiny hands clutching mine during bedtime stories! When did she grow up that fast? Time does fly."

Haitham smiled. "Yes, Sawsan, and one day you'll be a grandmother. Let's see about this dress issue. I hope it's not too indecent."

"Oh, Haitham, please don't spoil her special moment. She's sharing something that makes her happy with us. Just let it go. You know her. She can't have bought something too daring; she's conservative by nature. Please, Haitham, don't ruin her excitement."

"I'm happy to see her happy, but some things are unacceptable. Anyway, let's see the dress first before jumping to conclusions."

Allura walked out with a shy and innocent smile on her face, tip-toeing her way to the living room like a ballerina.

"Ta-da," she sang as she showed off her dress.

"Oh my little girl, you look like a princess," Sawsan said, her eyes sparkling as she took in just how stunning Allura looked.

"Hmmm, it's very nice, Allura. You look very beautiful," said Haitham in apprehension.

"Really, Daddy? You don't find it too short?"

"Well, it is short. But it's also elegant. I like it. Well done. Good choice," said Haitham, hiding his mixed feelings. "Who is going to be at that party, and what time are you coming back home?"

"Well, the party starts at six thirty, and all my friends are staying till midnight. It's a formal dress party by the beach."

Haitham gasped. "That's far too late, Allura. Midnight?"

"Please, Daddy. It'll be the last time I'll be able to see them," Allura begged.

"I don't know. How about ten?"

"Eleven?"

"Ten thirty and not one minute later."

"Fine. Thanks, Daddy!"

"Make sure you take your phone with you. Either your mother or I will call when we're on the way to pick you up."

"OK. Oh, I forgot. I got you both something too!" she said, rushing out.

"Allura! You didn't have to get us anything!" her mother called after her.

Returning in her pyjamas, Allura handed out the gift-wrapped packages.

"A DuPont wallet? Are you trying to hint you'll need more money with the move? You realise I won't be as rich once we leave Abu Dhabi?" joked Haitham.

"Allura, my love, you have such classy taste. I love the pendant. Thank you, darling! You didn't have to do that. The money I gave you, was for you. That's so considerate of you."

"It's the least I can do, with all you've done for me. You're about the best parents a girl can wish for."

Haitham and Sawsan were touched by her kind words and gesture.

"You're a good girl, Allura. I'm proud of you. The wallet will come in handy; perhaps it'll be your turn to fill it with some cash once we leave," her father teased.

As the living room filled with their laughter, the teenager felt better. Sure, things were about to change drastically, but she was confident that no matter what happened, they would be able to face it together.

Chapter 2

The Farewell Party

The big day had arrived, and Allura was getting ready for the party. As she fussed around, her mother walked in.

"Allura, would you like me to help you with your makeup?"

"Yes, please! I have no idea what half of this stuff is. The girls made me buy it," she said, gesturing to the myriad of products on her vanity.

Sawsan laughed.

"OK, darling. Settle down, let's see what we've got here."

They fell into a comfortable silence before Allura noticed her mother's wet eyes.

"Mum, why are you crying?"

"Tears of happiness, my love. I feel so proud that you're such a remarkable girl – well, no, you're a young lady now – and that there's so much waiting for you to experience and accomplish. Your life's just starting."

Allura started to tear up.

"Now none of that, you'll ruin your mascara," Sawsan reprimanded gently. "Now tell me, who are you trying to impress today?"

Allura giggled.

"Mum, you're sneaky! How did you know there was a boy?"

"You're my daughter. Of course I know. You think your mum is old-school? I may be old, but I wasn't born yesterday. So tell me all about him."

"His name is James. He's in my class. I have a huge crush on him. You know he told Helen that he'd like to take me out on a date sometime. But he never really asked me, and even if he did, I'm not sure I'd accept…"

"Well, Allura, nothing is wrong with having a crush on a boy. But make sure you have clear limits with him. Otherwise there'll be misunderstandings, and it may lead to problems. But I trust you'll make the right decisions when you feel you're ready to date and be in a relationship. So tell me more about James. Is he handsome?"

"Oh yes. He's got these long eyelashes and dreamy brown eyes. And his hair, oh my God, Mum, it looks so soft! He's very tall and fit from being in different sports clubs. Oh, and did I mention that we started to speak to one another in gym class? I was staring at him for so long that he actually approached me. He found it funny that I was so obvious," she said, giggling.

"Do you see him often?" asked Sawsan.

"Well, he's been in most of my classes since the first grade, so we have subjects in common and exchange eye contact all the time in school. I love him, Mum. He's just gorgeous."

Sawsan laughed. "Honey, you're only sixteen. This may feel like love for you now, but trust me, someday you'll look back at this whole thing and smile. But you know what? Enjoy the puppy love, and enjoy tonight. Voila, you're done."

Allura looked striking. Sawsan was great at applying makeup and knew exactly how to make her daughter shine.

Allura's eyes widened as she took in her transformation. The simple makeup helped add a soft, sensual look to her bronze complexion, complementing her loose, soft curls. Simple diamond stud earrings and a tennis bracelet completed the look, making her seem older than her teenage years.

Slipping into the silver sandals and grabbing the floral silver lace evening bag her friends had convinced her to buy the day before, Allura grabbed her phone and rushed to meet her friend, whose mother was driving them to the party.

"Mum, I have to go. I'm so nervous. I hope it's as great as I think it'll be," she said, brushing off imaginary dust from her dress.

"You'll have a great time. I feel it. Just enjoy it, and make sure you dance like no one is watching. Now go! It's getting late. Enjoy your time out. And remember, watch your back, and don't do anything I wouldn't do. Got it?"

Allura hugged her mother tightly.

"I don't know what I'd do without you. Love you!"

"Me too, darling. Don't forget to say goodbye to your father," Sawsan replied.

"Oh, I almost forgot!"

Allura ran to the kitchen, where Haitham was busy fixing himself a peanut butter sandwich, and kissed him goodbye.

"Take care, pumpkin. Don't forget, either Mum or I will be there to pick you up at ten thirty. Have a great time," Haitham said, smiling.

"Sure, Daddy. Love you! Bye!" Allura called out as she walked out of the front door. She couldn't wait to see the reaction on James's face. Allura paused to check her appearance in the elevator mirror one last time. She was ready to party.

Upon arriving to the party, she was greeted by everyone as she made her way around the venue. Balloons, candles, and flowers surrounded the beach as the music played in the background. Everyone was dancing and enjoying the night. James had still not arrived, but Allura wasn't worried. She was enjoying the night anyway.

An hour later, Maria ran up to Allura and excitedly whispered in her ear, "Guess who's here?"

It was James. As he approached Allura, she froze. She felt butterflies in her stomach and didn't know how to react.

"Hi, Allura," James said with a grin. "So you're the party girl tonight. All this is for you, huh?"

Allura giggled shyly. "Yeah, I guess!"

"It's a bit noisy. How about we take a short walk?" he suggested.

"Sure!"

James and Allura started to talk as they strolled along the shore. They spoke about school, how they met, what they'd miss once Allura was gone, and their future plans.

"Do you know what I like most about you, Allura? You're beautiful, yet so down-to-earth. You're also probably the smartest girl I know and always happy to help everyone around you. Not to mention, you're the best swimmer I know. I'm going to miss seeing you around."

As he spoke, Allura's throat started to tighten, and her palms grew sweaty. She thought to herself, *Is this when it starts? Is this how it goes? Is he going to kiss me now, or am I supposed to make that first move?* She was speechless and had no idea what to say or how to respond.

"Allura?"

"Yes, James?"

"What's wrong? Did I say something wrong?"

"No, I'm just speechless; I don't know what to say. You're too kind."

James smiled softly as he reached out to hold Allura's hand and kiss it. "Everything I said was true. You're a wonderful person, and I am blessed and honoured to have met you."

"James, why did you wait to tell me all this at my farewell party? I've known you since we were in preschool. Now, you're suddenly telling me all this when I'm about to leave for another country."

"You never really gave me the chance to speak to you, Allura. You were always busy with your homework, at swimming rehearsals or with your friends. When I tried to approach you for a date, you didn't show that you were interested. So how and when could I have possibly expressed my feelings towards you?"

Allura knew deep down that James was right and wondered what step to take from here. She was confused. Should she encourage a kiss, or should she keep it simple, cut the conversation short, and join in with the rest of her friends at the party? She had promised her mother that she would behave, yet she was curious about how that first kiss would feel. She decided to suggest joining in with the rest of the crowd and leaving things to flow.

"I love that song. Do you want to dance?" she quickly suggested.

"Yeah, I like it too. I'd love to dance; I'll just grab myself a drink and come back. Would you like to drink anything?" asked James, relieved to get out of the suddenly awkward situation.

"I'm good, thank you; I'll wait for you on the dance floor."

As Allura approached her friends by the dance floor, they all stopped, waiting for her to spill the juicy details. Helen grabbed her shoulders and yelled, "So, what's going on? Did he kiss you yet?"

"Helen, is that all you think about? No, he didn't kiss me. What's wrong with you? We just spoke. He's walking towards us, so stop! Besides, that was loud," Allura replied in a mock-angry tone.

"OK, whatever, sorry. Go back to your lover boy," Helen replied teasingly before shoving her in James's direction.

"Helen! Watch it!"

Allura turned around at the sound of chuckling. James held out his hand.

"May I have this dance?"

Allura blushed. She was going to deal with her friends later.

"Um, sure," she said shyly.

She began to dance, letting the music's hypnotising rhythm take over her body. Suddenly she felt James hug her waist, causing an astounding shiver to course down the length of her spine.

"What are you doing?" she asked, confused.

"I'm hugging my girl. Am I not allowed to?"

"Ha-ha, so I'm your girl now? Whatever, let's dance."

Allura and James danced away till the music started to slow down. James grabbed her arms and placed them around his neck. He held Allura close and kissed her softly and repeatedly on her forehead and around her lips and cheeks. He was teasing her, and she enjoyed every bit of it. She felt his breath all over her face, which gave her the shivers. Her body started to steam up, a feeling she had never felt before. She decided to relax and relish the moment, praying her parents wouldn't walk in on them anytime soon.

"You're beautiful, Allura," James kept repeating as they danced away.

Even though it wasn't the actual kiss she envisioned or had in mind, Allura was excited and happy with how things went that night. The moment she shared with James was very special and sentimental; she was going to remember and treasure it for the rest of her life.

Suddenly, she startled, causing James to look at her in concern.

"What time is it?" she asked, fumbling for her phone. Her heart sank. It was eleven fifteen, and she was nearly an hour over curfew. On top of that, she had forgotten to call her parents.

"Oh my God, James, it's eleven fifteen already. That's nearly an hour after my curfew! I need to call my parents now!"

"Chill out, you sound like Cinderella all of a sudden." He tried to calm her down by turning the sudden anxiety into a joke, but that didn't seem to work. "OK, well, how can I help?"

"Sorry, James. Just gimme a second!"

Allura picked up her phone and to her surprise found no missed calls from her parents. She then attempted to phone them, but neither mobile phone was switched on, which made her even more worried.

"Something's wrong. It's not like my parents not to phone me or check up on me at all like that, especially since I'm this late." Allura was speaking to all her friends, who at that point were gathered at the party's entrance, ready to go home.

"I can drop you home, Allura. Don't worry, I'm sure they're fine," said James.

"No, no, I'll keep trying. One sec, let me try calling them again."

After a few more failed attempts, Allura grew even more concerned. Deciding to catch a ride back home with Helen,

Allura prayed that it was just a case of her parents forgetting to charge their phones.

Having sent Helen and her mother away with promises of contacting them with any updates, Allura felt a sense of foreboding as she rode the elevator to her apartment.

Walking down the corridor, Allura was surprised to find the front door already wide open and her next-door neighbour sitting on their couch.

"Auntie Lucy, good evening. What are you doing here? Where are Mum and Dad? What is it, is something wrong?" she asked fearfully.

Lucy Duarte was a Portuguese art designer who lived with her husband next door. Her husband, Flavio, was Haitham's boss. The families were close enough to have exchanged emergency contacts and apartment keys. They had been neighbours and best friends for the past ten years, and Lucy and Flavio were considered as practically family by the Mahmouds.

"Honey, take a seat. You need to sit down."

It was confirmed. Allura knew something was wrong. She felt herself start to hyperventilate.

"Auntie Lucy, what is it? Where are Mum and Dad? What's going on? They were supposed to pick me up from my party, and no one called or showed up. Auntie, what is it? Please, please, tell me!"

Allura's eyes began to tear up as she waited impatiently for the news about the two people closest to her heart.

Chapter 3

Life Changing

Allura kept hoping and praying that everything was fine and that her paranoid mind was playing games with her. As she looked at her neighbour, who remained silent, as though trying to find the right words, it felt like the longest five seconds of her life.

"Auntie Lucy, please talk to me! What happened to Mum and Dad? I'm going crazy here!"

Allura started to cry. She knew something was wrong but kept hoping that she might be imagining it.

Lucy took a deep breath and spoke calmly. Although she tried her best to hide her feelings, it was evident from her expression that something was terribly wrong.

"Allura, your parents were on their way to surprise you at the farewell party. They were meant to attend the last part of it and had a speech prepared for you. Honey, they got into an accident, and—"

"And what, Auntie Lucy? Where are they now?" screamed Allura.

She got down on her knees and crawled towards the older woman, placing her head on Lucy's lap. Lucy began to cry as she ran her fingers through Allura's hair.

"I am so sorry, Allura."

Allura stood up, wiping her face. "What do you mean you're sorry? Tell me, where are my parents?" she asked sharply.

Haitham and Sawsan had been on their way to Allura's farewell party. They had a cake, presents and a speech prepared for her. No-one but the party organisers knew about their plan.

Haitham's sports car went up in flames due to a flammable liquid getting into contact with some frayed wiring within the engine. Haitham had the habit of locking all the doors in the car before hitting the road. When he and Sawsan tried to unlock the doors, they couldn't open them fast enough. The fire brigade and police were on the scene within minutes, but it was too late. They were pronounced dead on the scene, and their remains were airlifted to a nearby hospital.

Lucy learned about the whole incident when the police tracked them down using Haitham's licence plate numbers. In his profile, Haitham had listed Flavio as his emergency contact.

Lucy hugged the trembling teenager as she told her about her parents' unfortunate accident. She explained that her parents loved her very much and only wished the best for her. For Allura's sake, she tried hard to maintain a calm tone despite being highly emotional and saddened by the incident herself.

"Allura, I know this won't make you feel any better, but your mum and dad will always be with you, spiritually, emotionally and mentally. They are in a better place, and you will always have us, your family back in Egypt and all your friends. No one will leave you alone. You are not alone, Allura. You…"

Lucy broke down in tears as she hugged Allura tightly. She was grieving and couldn't hold that back any longer.

"I'm sorry, Allura. I am supposed to be the one easing your pain, and now I'm the one crying." Lucy gasped as she drew Allura closer, as though terrified the teenager would also disappear.

Sawsan and Haitham were very dear to her heart and had helped the couple through some difficult times. Flavio was twenty years older than Lucy, which resulted in a lot of miscommunication between the couple. The Mahmouds were always offering advice and calming them both down whenever they got into an argument.

Another thing that caused Lucy and Sawsan to bond was Lucy's troubles conceiving a child. She was thirty-one years old, while Flavio was fifty-six. They went to several doctors, but to no avail, which was what mainly caused the tension between them.

"Allura, you are the child I never had. You are like my daughter. I know it's too early to speak about this, but Uncle Flavio and I would be more than happy to have you stay with us if you chose to. Honey, for now, I want you to take your time with all of this until your mind is clearer. Then you can decide on what it is you want to do, and we are here to help you. We plan to contact your father's aunt in Egypt. She's an elderly woman who lives alone, and your mother always mentioned that if anything ever happened to your parents, your Aunt Nahed would be a perfect option, since she lives alone and misses the company. I was told she's a very sweet and loving woman."

Allura suddenly pushed Lucy away.

"Stop it! Stop talking. And stop crying. Ugh, stop squeezing me that way! What's wrong with you? You're a liar. My parents are still alive! Just before I went to the party, Mum was talking about always being there for me, no matter what! You're a liar!"

Allura started to feel nauseous. She was in a daze. The bereaved teenager felt a tremendous amount of guilt. There were things she still needed to say to her parents and things she needed to hear them say. She had been looking forward to coming back home and having her usual girlie chat with her Mum about the amazing party organised for her and about the special moments she shared with James. She had also looked forward to snuggling up with both her parents in their bed, which she usually did every night before bedtime.

"I'm going to be sick," Allura groaned before rushing to the bathroom, where she threw up forcefully and wailed in despair. Lucy was right beside her the whole time, patting her back and reminding her that as hard as it seemed now, with time, the pain would heal. She kept encouraging her to cry and let it out.

Meanwhile, Flavio was at the hospital finishing necessary paperwork for the Mahmouds. Their remains were to be transported to Egypt, where they were scheduled to be buried. His only thought was to make sure Allura was offered the best support and help possible. He knew that she needed time and patience to grieve in her own way. He had already spoken to Lucy about it, and they had both agreed that they were not going to leave Allura unless she chose to move back to Egypt, as originally planned by her parents.

Flavio was determined to sue the manufacturer of the car that Haitham was driving. He felt that the money he could gather from suing the company should go to Allura. He was concerned about her financial stability, though he knew that Haitham had a carefully planned savings account that he had opened for his daughter.

At the Mahmouds' home, Lucy had prepared some hot chamomile tea for Allura, who refused to drink or eat anything or even talk at that point. Lucy tried to comfort her as best she could, but Allura was shaking and had become withdrawn as tears ran heavily down her face. She was distraught. What she had expected to be one of the best nights of her life had ended up being the worst.

"Allura, drink your tea. It will help you relax a little bit. Darling, can you please speak to me? Say something. Anything. Please just talk to me."

Allura was silent as the tears kept running down her face. All she could think of was how her parents must have felt during the accident and right before they took their last breath. She wondered why God would do that to her, but at the same time felt comforted that her parents were safe in His embrace. She felt that she needed to be strong, so her parents wouldn't be sad. She knew they were near her somehow. Allura had always believed that the calmer and more civilised a person is about a loved one dying, the easier the transition would be for the person who had just passed, and so it was selfish to scream or overreact. She believed that doing so could actually hurt their souls.

I have to be strong, she kept thinking and saying to herself. *Mummy always told me she'd be here for me. Daddy always called me his baby diamond and was proud of me. I have to be strong. I have to be strong.*

"Allura? Would you like to spend the night in our place? It might be hard staying here after…" suggested Lucy tentatively.

"Huh? No, I'm going to sleep on my parents' bed. You go, Auntie Lucy. I need to speak to Mummy and Daddy tonight. I really do need some alone time, please."

"Allura, I won't leave you. If you don't want to come over to our place tonight and would like to spend the night here, I'll be right by your side. If you want to sleep on your parents' bed, I'll sleep on the floor, if that's all right with you."

"No, Auntie Lucy, go home to Uncle Flavio. I'll be fine. Thank you."

Meanwhile, Allura's phone did not stop ringing. James, Helen and several other concerned friends were calling to make sure everything was fine.

"Would you like me to answer your friends? Your phone hasn't stopped ringing, they seem worried about you."

"No! I don't want to speak to anyone, please. Switch off my phone, and leave me alone, please!"

Allura didn't sleep a wink that night. She kept smelling their scent on their pillows and bed sheet. She'd occasionally weep, laugh and even giggle. It all depended on the things that came to her mind and the moments she would remember.

Lucy insisted on sleeping on the floor near Allura. She teared up as she witnessed the girl's different reactions, but did her best to stay quiet. She knew Allura needed her alone time while saying her last goodbyes to her parents. After all, crying and laughing were both a way of healing.

Once Lucy sensed that Allura had started to get drowsy, she decided to phone Flavio to let him know she'd sleep in the Mahmouds' residence tonight.

"Hello, Lucy. How is Allura?"

"How do you think she is, Flavio? Terrible. She's terrified, poor child. I'm trying so hard to comfort her, but there's very little comforting that can be done, given the situation."

"That's only normal. Well, listen, I am done with the hospital paperwork and the transportation details. We're due to fly their bodies down to Egypt early tomorrow morning. I need you to help prepare Allura for that trip. I know it's way too soon for her, but she needs to be kept in the loop on everything from now on. Unfortunately, the child has been forced to grow up too early."

"Yes, Flavio, I understand. I'm not sure how I'm going to break it to her. She's vulnerable right now. I'll speak to her in the morning, or later during the night if I feel she's ready to hear about this. What are your plans now?"

"I'm going to come back home and make some phone calls. I will call her Aunt Nahed and ask her to prepare a room for Allura, just in case she decides to move back to Egypt. Have you spoken to her about this?"

"Well, I tried to explain the situation, but she's in no state to make up her mind right now about anything. She's in severe shock."

"I completely understand. Well, Lucy, we have to be strong and patient. This is not easy, and it won't get any easier."

Flavio went back home and phoned Nahed, who was devastated by the news, but forced herself to focus on Allura and her welfare. She was understanding and comforting and told Flavio that the burial arrangements were under control, that he shouldn't worry, and to only think of being there for Allura till they all arrived safely.

Nahed was on a mission to take in Allura for as long as she wanted to stay. She was eager to hear that Allura may consider moving in with her and prepared herself accordingly.

Nahed was Haitham's youngest and favourite aunt. She lived in an upper-class area of Cairo called Zamalek. Her mansion was beautiful; the front porch was a little oasis off the street overlooking the Nile River where she normally sipped her afternoon tea, or invited friends or neighbours to spend time over a chat. There was a certain ease at the mid-century house, which she had inherited from her mother. She made it a point to water her colourful garden herself on a daily basis. It was covered with exotic plants and flowers in various pots, along with small trees and shrubs dotting the landscape.

The interior was elegant, and there was plenty of space to accommodate guests and family. The eclectic and highly personal home also featured an old attic where she kept most of the books and antiques that she had inherited. They were priceless, and she always made sure the books were neatly stacked in the lime-coloured mahogany bookshelf, and the antiques kept spotless.

She treated her butler, chef and two cleaners with the utmost respect and generosity. Her house was always well taken care of, despite the fact that it was prone to attracting dust and fleas due to its riverfront location.

Nahed's home was her kingdom. Every single antique, piece of furniture and flower pot meant a lot to her, and reminded her of how much life surrounded her, although she lived alone.

The elderly woman felt she lived a fulfilling, busy life. Allura moving in with her, however, would fill a void in her heart. Nahed felt that she and Allura would bond easily, if the teenager was anything like the charming woman she had met all those years ago in London. She still smiled fondly at how Sawsan made Haitham blush at the slightest things.

Upon receiving the news, Nahed instructed her cleaners to prepare the second master bedroom for Allura. She then decided to go shopping and buy all the things she felt would be necessary for the young woman.

Nahed then phoned one of her friends, a distant relative who worked as a family counsellor. He was mostly involved with helping couples who were looking to separate or family members who had lost a loved one, similar to Allura's situation.

"Hello, Alaa, how are you?"

"Nahed? My dear Nahed, is that you?"

"Yes, Alaa, it's me. How have you been?"

"I'm very well, thank you. How about yourself? You don't sound too good, not to mention that you haven't phoned me in ages. I hope everything is all right?"

"Do you remember my nephew Haitham and his wife Sawsan?"

"Of course I do – lovely couple. They now live in the UK, right?"

"No, actually they moved from the UK years ago. They live in Abu Dhabi. Well, lived. An unfortunate incident happened, and they got into a car accident and passed away yesterday."

"I am so sorry to hear that, Nahed. That's awful. My deepest condolences. I will pray for them. How are you taking this? I know they both meant a lot to you."

"To be honest with you, Alaa, I don't know how I'm taking this. I think I'm still in denial. Maybe that's because all I can think about right now is their sixteen-year-old daughter, Allura. She was their only child, and she's got no one but me now. She's coming to live with me, possibly forever!"

"Wow, that's big news! And you want to know how to deal with all of this. Am I right?"

"Yes, Alaa, exactly. I need your help. I need to know what to do. I am honestly terrified with the responsibility, and I don't know if I can actually help her deal with this traumatic situation. How can you help a child who's just lost both her parents in one go? How can you explain to her that it's all about fate without having her question things? I'm just very anxious, and I need your guidance and professional support. What do I do, Alaa? You're a dear friend and a reputable family counsellor. I know you've got plenty of experience with situations such as this one. Can you help me?"

"Of course, I'll help you, Nahed. What are you talking about? You are more than a friend; you are family and a very dear person to me. I also have great respect for Haitham, God rest his soul, and knowing that she's his daughter makes me want to help even more. Please consider this taken care of. I want you to calm down and work on yourself till Allura comes. Can you pay me a visit me this evening?"

"Yes, of course I can. That would be great. I definitely need to speak with someone who can advise me on what steps to take from here. Alaa, I'm not getting any younger. I don't even know if I'll be able to get along with Allura. She's only sixteen! And I've never met her."

"My dear Nahed, calm down. You will be just fine. You're a fine lady, young at heart and very intelligent. Of course you'll get along with her. As you rightly put it, you're all she's got, so she'll be attached to you in no time. I just need you to be patient and take things one day at a time. Allow her to mourn in her own way; you must expect some anger from her at first. All you can do right now is to listen to her when she's ready to open up. When is she due to arrive?"

"Well, she's accompanying her parents on the plane early tomorrow morning, and they are due to be buried immediately after they arrive. So, obviously I have no time to prepare myself for all of this. Suddenly my life is changing right before my eyes!"

As much as she felt empathetic for Allura, deep down, Nahed knew that it was time to say goodbye to her current lifestyle, and knew she was going to miss it. She had no obligations, no strings attached, and no drama to deal with. Suddenly she was about to take on this huge responsibility of caring for a sixteen-year-old whom she knew nothing about. She felt bad for feeling this way, but couldn't help but worry about the new life being forced on her.

Chapter 4

Change is Never Easy

Allura insisted on attending her parents' funeral. Flavio, Lucy and Nahed were by her side as she witnessed the burial arrangements in detail. She was advised to appear once the bodies were already buried and pray for her parents, but Allura was adamant that she wanted to be with her parents throughout the whole process, till the last second.

Nahed admired her strength and was instantly attached to Allura. The girl reminded her of Sawsan, who was intelligent and strong, yet sensitive and delicate. Right after the burial, Nahed didn't hesitate to invite Allura to be a part of her life. She wanted to be natural and spontaneous around her, especially after witnessing what type of person she was.

"Allura, I know you've been through a lot and that it's very hard to take a decision right now. But I would like to invite you to be part of my life, to move in with me and make up for the emptiness I have in my life. It would be an honour and a pleasure to have you, and I promise that I'll treat you as my own daughter," said Nahed as they walked out of the graveyard.

In the meantime, Lucy and Flavio extended their own invitation to host Allura in their home. "Sweetheart, as we told you from the beginning, you are more than welcome to stay with us in Abu Dhabi. We can even move to another city, like Dubai, for example, so that you can try to move on with your life faster. We'll make the necessary arrangements. We'd love you to be a part of our family, Allura. But ultimately, you need to decide what would make you happy."

Allura remembered her mother's words about how important it is to strengthen one's ties with family, and at the end of the day Aunt Nahed was considered family. She politely turned down Flavio and Lucy's offer, and thanked them for all their support and help, promising that she'd stay in touch, and possibly visit them when the time felt right.

"Thank you, Aunt Nahed. I do hope that I won't be a burden. I've heard a lot about our family here, and would like to get to know you better," said Allura.

Nahed hugged her before gently caressing Allura's cheeks. "My beautiful child, you won't regret this. You have just made an old woman very happy. Welcome to my world, my love. God rest their souls, I'm sure you've put your parents' souls at ease just now."

Not long after the burial, Nahed enrolled Allura in a well-reputed British curriculum school close to her home. Most of the pupils enrolled there came from wealthy backgrounds, since it was one of the most expensive schools in Cairo.

Allura's parents had left her a huge lump sum of savings, and she'd inherited several properties. Haitham owned a house in the United Kingdom that was rented out, a condo in California, a two-bedroom apartment in Dubai and a beach house on the North Coast in Alexandria. His company was in the midst of preparing a death pension and additional savings to pass on to his family. Flavio was in talks with the manufacturer of Haitham's car to try to secure some sort of compensation due to what was referred to in the official police report as 'a definite fault with the car'.

The Mahmouds had always looked out for Allura's welfare, since they were concerned about her being a single child. They had everything planned and well-organised for her in case of an emergency, and Flavio was a trusted friend whom Haitham was certain would take care of Allura in times of need.

It was already Allura's seventh day in Cairo, and she had asked her aunt to give her an extra two weeks before she could start school again. She wasn't ready to take part in a daily routine. She was confused, sad, angry and frustrated with everything that had happened, and above all, she missed her parents and her old life deeply.

Nahed was considerate with Allura, which made the transition easier for her; she was already comfortable spending time at Nahed's house, but still needed her alone time.

"Good morning, sleepy face! Wake up, we're going swimming!"

It was seven-thirty on a Sunday morning. Allura had only just gone to bed an hour before. She hadn't been able to sleep all night. She had suffered from major insomnia since the accident, sleeping less than three hours a night, if at all.

"What time is it?" asked Allura grumpily, as her eyes fought to stay closed.

"It's time to go for a fresh, nice swim. It's lovely and sunny outside," said Nahed as she pulled the curtains wide open to let in light. "It's just perfect for a day out! So get out of bed, lazy pants!"

Despite reminding herself of what Dr Alaa advised her to do – "Let her be, wait till she comes to you" – Nahed was anxious to help Allura snap out of her depression. Seeing the girl this subdued and unhappy worried her a great deal.

"Auntie, I don't want to go for a swim. It's very early, and I haven't slept all night. Please close those curtains and leave me alone."

As she surveyed the room, Nahed looked up at Allura. "Sheesh, Allura, look how untidy this room is. You need a definite change of atmosphere. You can't stay cooped up in this untidy room forever. Come on now. We'll go to the social centre for a swim. Then, I'll take you out for lunch and a movie."

"Auntie Nahed, please. I don't want to go out, I don't want to see people and I don't want anything in life. Just leave me alone!" yelled Allura. She then placed a pillow over her head and covered her whole body with the blanket. "Please just leave."

Nahed was devastated. She thought she was helping Allura by suggesting fun activities. She felt slightly offended by Allura's tone of voice, but kept reminding herself of the teenager's challenging situation. She rolled her tongue ten times before she decided to answer back.

"Fine, Allura, take your time. I'm here if you change your mind. Rest now."

Stepping out of the bedroom, she called her dear friend.

"What did I do wrong, Alaa?"

"You've done everything wrong! Didn't I tell you to let her be, especially at the beginning? Put yourself in her shoes. You just lost both your parents, and an elderly aunt, who you knew nothing about in your past life, suddenly decides to wake you up after what was probably a restless night with little sleep. Would you have liked that to happen to you?"

Nahed pursed her lips. Alaa was right, but she still felt as though there was more she could do. Finally, she relented. "Alaa, I want her to snap out of this. What do I do now?"

"Nothing, just leave her alone. She'll come to you when she's ready. Simply ask her if she'd like to eat when it's time for meals. That's it. Other than that, check up on her to make sure she's fine without her noticing. Don't be pushy, Nahed."

"I've got it. I won't be pushy. But I'm afraid she'll do something to herself. The girl won't sleep, eat or talk. She's subdued and so quiet. She hardly cried during her parents' funeral. Is that even normal?"

"Yes, it is. Everything is normal in a situation like this. People react differently. Our fingers are not alike, Nahed. She is mourning in her own way, and you are meant to allow her to mourn. Please do not push her, and do not assume things on her behalf. As long as you're checking up on her in order to ensure she's safe and hasn't done something stupid, you'll both be fine!"

After speaking to Dr Alaa, Nahed decided to move on with her life the way it used to be before Allura had arrived. Perhaps she really was being overly pushy and anxious. All she had thought about since the incident had been Allura. Any other activities had been put on hold. But that was about to change.

Four days later, Nahed invited a few of her friends over for a barbecue. They all gathered at the backyard patio, as the beautiful sounds of old, classical French music played in the background.

The chef was preparing mouth-watering barbecued chicken, meat and vegetables, as five of Nahed's lifelong friends sipped on their wine, ate some snacks, and laughed the evening away.

"Do you remember when Farid stopped Nahed at the social club a few years ago and reminded her who he was? Poor soul, he was blushing like a little child. He was like, 'You haven't changed one bit, Nahed, and you're still as beautiful as a white, fresh rose.' What a romantic he was!" said Hania, one of Nahed's bubbly friends.

Once a week, the same circle of ladies sat and ate, played cards, listened to music and reminisced about the past. The group gathered frequently at Nahed's house, since it was the most spacious.

Farid was a funny fellow with a twitch. He had loved Nahed since they were younger. He had proposed to her a few times, but Nahed was simply not interested in remarrying after her husband passed away.

"Oh please, Hania, I can't believe you still remember that story," said Nahed, laughing. "I find this old, bald man walking up to me and comparing me to a beautiful white rose. I hadn't recognised him at all. I was shocked and asked who the hell he was. When he reminded me of his name, I still didn't recall who he was, till he reminded me in detail, which is exactly when I couldn't help but tell him off!"

"What did you tell him exactly? You probably hurt his feelings like you normally do, you awful woman," joked Laila.

"I told the old man to get a life and get over me already. I asked him to go back home to his beloved wife and leave the beautiful, ageing rose alone, but of course I spoke with humour. I was just joking! I felt bad when he told me his wife had passed years ago and that he had never forgotten me."

"You're just describing half of what happened. Tell them what you said next," said Hania.

"Well, the man wouldn't give up, and I was desperate to change topics. So I asked him what he's been up to lately to have aged so much! His skin was frail and wrinkly, and his bald head looked like his hair had just been shaved off by a lawnmower! I was in shock. He was very handsome when we were younger!"

"Oh my God, Nahed, did you actually tell him all that to his face? Poor man!" chortled Gladdis.

"No, silly, I'm telling you how I felt. I just said he looked old. The whole conversation turned into a complete joke anyway, and he was laughing it off too. But to be honest, deep down inside I was sad for him. He looked like a changed man; life took its toll on him, by the looks of it."

"And what's pathetic, yet hilarious, is that after everything she told him, he still had a ridiculous smirk on his face. He didn't care less about her inconsiderate reaction; all he cared about was that Nahed, the actual Nahed, was right there in front of him. Besides, she's not telling you half the story. The woman's becoming forgetful. Nahed, you've become senile, love," said Hania with a chuckle.

"Me? Senile? Look at you! You've had artificial teeth since you turned fifty, and get the few hair follicles that are left on your head dyed every week! You're the last to speak about senility, you grey-crowned crane!"

The ladies' loud laughter drifted through the house, piquing Allura's interest from where she lay in her room. She was intrigued to know what was going on, as she hadn't heard this much laughter in ages.

She tip-toed her way down to the kitchen to check what the fuss was about, her stomach growling as she took in the smell of grilled chicken and flavoured marinated meat. She was also intrigued by the cheerful music that drifted across the patio. Allura had always loved listening to music, with a particular preference for classical music and opera.

As she approached Nahed and her friends, Allura suddenly remembered what a mess she was. She hadn't brushed her hair or teeth, or even taken a bath, for at least several days. She decided to go back upstairs to freshen up, but then Gladdis spotted her.

"Well, hello there! Are you the famous Allura? Nahed, look who's here. It's our Allura!"

"Uh, hello," said Allura shyly, as she tried to fix her hair as fast as possible.

"Oh my God, are you barefoot, young lady? Wow, you are a wild one, aren't you?" cackled Hania, pointing her nearly empty wine glass towards Allura.

"Oh, I'm sorry. I'll just go upstairs and…"

"No, no, no! Don't go anywhere; I'm happy you're barefoot. You're a free soul, my love. Your aunt needs company like you. She's too constipated. By six in the morning, she's fully made up and dressed up as though she's going to the office. I have no idea why she even bothers, given the fact that she's never worked a day in her entire life, yet never hesitates to wear her high heels and fancy designer suits," added Hania.

"Oh shut it, Hania. Don't listen to her, Allura. She's just sloshed! How are you feeling, love?" asked Nahed with a warm smile.

A small smile lit Allura's face, much to Nahed's relief. It appeared that the young lady was finally starting to relax. She found Nahed's friends entertaining.

"Honey, you must be starving. Would you like to eat with us? Oh, how rude of me. I almost forgot to introduce you to my friends. This is Hania, she thinks she's funny, but she's just an old drunk who laughs at her own silly jokes. And this is Gladdis, I've known her since we were in school; she's my ultimate soul mate. Laila is our lady, always dressed to impress, and this lovely woman is Heidi – she's a successful writer and a businesswoman. Everyone, meet my beautiful Allura."

"Hello, Allura!" the women chorused.

"Hey! How come I'm the only one you described negatively? Have I not been with you through thick and thin? Literally, I might add," Hania said, irritated.

Nahed rolled her eyes and continued speaking to Allura. "Ignore her. She won't stop. We always pick on each other that way, but in the end she's my love. I adore Hania."

Extending her hands to reach out for the chair next to her, Nahed asked Allura to join them.

"Hello everyone, pleasure to meet you all. Well, I'll go change and be back in a bit, if that's OK?"

"Sure, honey, we're waiting for you. Take your time," said Nahed.

"Allura, we're honestly very hungry. You have eight minutes to shower, dress and come down, and you'd better come down barefoot again," said Hania, with a giggle.

Allura rushed upstairs and freshened up in record time. She suddenly felt warmth around her. She was happy to sense friendliness again after isolating herself for so long. She was still under severe shock from everything that had happened to her, but felt herself slowly start to snap out of it. She remembered a lot of what her mother used to say to her. Sawsan always spoke to her about being strong during difficult times and how challenging life could get. Sawsan and Allura weren't just mother and child; they were friends. She worried about Allura, who was, like Sawsan herself, sensitive and naive. She followed her heart quite a lot.

That afternoon, Nahed's friends put in an extra effort to distract Allura. They spoke about memories, and wouldn't stop bickering with each other. They were very close, and no one ever took offence to anything that was said. It was all taken lightly and in good spirits.

Allura loved the atmosphere and joined in when everyone started playing cards later on in the evening. She was interested in spending more time with the group, which pleased Nahed tremendously. She was delighted to see Allura's brighter side begin to appear.

By the end of the evening, Nahed and Allura exchanged their goodbyes as they dropped the ladies at the front door. When all the guests were gone, Nahed looked at Allura and extended her arms. "Can I hug you, Allura?"

"You remind me of Mum, Auntie. She loved hugging me."

"Well, what can I say, missy? You are huggable material. Come here, you! I've longed for that hug."

Nahed held Allura's chin up to maintain eye contact with her. "Allura, I know you've been through a very rough time. I won't say I understand what you're going through, because I don't. I can't imagine what it must feel like for a sixteen-year-old to lose both her parents at once. But I do know one thing. You are starting to take baby steps towards feeling better, and that makes me very proud of you. You're a strong-willed child, and I am fortunate to have you as part of my life."

"Thank you, Auntie Nahed, and I am sorry if I was unpleasant these past few days. It's one thing to lose both your parents in one go, and another to live with an old woman you've never met before. No offence, but honestly, I don't know what to expect."

"It's only normal to feel confused, angry and resentful at this stage. Just work on getting through this tough time, for your own sake. As for this old woman, well, rest assured, I'm not so bad – at least, I hope I'm not," said Nahed with a smile. "I want you to know that I am always going to be here for you. This is not easy on me either, but together, you and I will get through. We'll be all right."

Allura nodded in agreement and put her head down. Tears started to cloud her vision. "I know, Auntie, but I miss Mum and Dad. It's so hard. I feel so alone, and I don't know what to do. I didn't even get the chance to say goodbye."

"Now, now, Allura, we'll have no such talk about feeling alone. As long as I'm alive, you will never be alone. Take it one day at a time, and allow yourself to mourn for as long as it takes. All what you're going through is normal." Nahed had remembered Dr Alaa's advice and decided to share some of his wisdom with Allura.

"Don't think of tomorrow. Think getting by for now, today. Just take it step by step, and things will fall in place. I'm not saying you'll forget about what happened to your

Mum and Dad. That will never happen. But you'll learn to accept things and move on. Think about it. What more could happen? The worst has already happened, and you're going to overcome it. From here onwards, you can face any obstacle that stands in your way."

Allura was astounded at Nahed's candour, yet she respected it. Her words were real and from the heart. But Allura was thinking deep down inside that it was best not to allow herself to get too close to Nahed in case she was next in line. "But Auntie, you're old too. What if—"

"What if I die? Well, as awful as that may sound, if I die, you'll become extremely rich." Nahed laughed. "I know it's not the right time to discuss this, but I've decided to add you to my will alongside Sam, my son in Canada. Not to mention the fact that Flavio is working on getting you money from your father's insurance company as well as from the car company, because they believe there was a fault with the car itself. I know it's not the time to speak about any of this, but I just want you to know that you're financially covered for life – and after life, even! So you have nothing to worry about. Money is security, and you have the money now. You're a brave child; I know you'll be just fine."

"What's the use of money if it won't bring back Mum and Dad?"

"Well, it will help safeguard your future and get you on your two beautiful feet. You need to think of what's next for you. You need to focus on finishing school and then entering university and becoming as successful as your parents. Don't you want to make them proud?"

"I don't know what I want, but I do know that Mum wanted all that for me too. Just before she died she spoke of those exact things, university, my career, and the future, as if she knew…"

"You will know what you want with time. The older we get the wiser we become, and with age comes direction. You will find your path eventually, Allura. Like I said, take things minute by minute, hour by hour and day by day. Now tell me, would you like to join me in the television room? My favourite series has just started. I watch it every night. We can binge on popcorn!"

The television room was located on the second floor. Along with an old television set that Nahed didn't have the heart to replace, the room was filled with various souvenirs and family pictures. She also had some of her favourite indoor plants around, in keeping with her preference to be surrounded by nature as much as possible.

"I wouldn't mind watching some television, it's been a while since I've done that. I'll skip on the popcorn, though. I'm completely full. The barbecue was absolutely yummy."

"Bon appétit! You need to eat better. You've lost quite a lot of weight lately, and that's not good. You need to regain your strength. I tell you what, I've got an even better idea. Has your mum ever spoken to you about her romance with your father?"

Allura sat up in curiosity. "How do you mean?"

"I mean, do you know about how your parents initially met? Did they ever tell you?"

"No. I've always wondered, though."

Nahed settled down on the couch, patting the empty space beside her.

"Then maybe we should ditch the movie idea after all. Come, sit next to me. Now, let me see. It was a warm, sunny day in London…"

Chapter 5

A Chance Encounter

It was a fine Saturday morning, filled with light breezes and warm, sunny skies. Sawsan decided to take advantage of the weather and head for a relaxing stroll to her favourite teashop, the Garden Café located within Regent's Park, close to the famous Regent's University, in north-west London.

Settling down, she reached into her satchel and began working on her doctoral research papers with a cup of piping hot tea at her fingertips. She had a lot of work to finish off and quickly became engrossed in the documents.

Sawsan's concentration was interrupted when a man stumbled into her table. In the ruckus, her cup wobbled. But Sawsan's quick reflexes saved her papers from their impending, soggy doom.

"I'm so sorry! I'm such a klutz. I didn't mean to spill your tea," said the man embarrassedly. "Amazing reflexes though," he continued, gesturing to the cup clutched tightly in her hand.

"Well, it's fine. You're lucky my papers weren't affected. Otherwise, I would have definitely given you a piece of my mind," Sawsan said, smiling.

Suddenly, a sparrow landed on the table. "Oh, look at you, you little cute thing! Where did you come from?" she spoke to the little bird as she caressed it gently.

"That's remarkable! I've been chasing that same bird all around the café, thus the reason why I carelessly stumbled into you like that. I think it's lost its way. My aunt and I saw it flying around, and I thought to myself, why not help it find its way to freedom?" he said.

Standing up with the bird safely tucked away between her hands, they made their way towards the garden outside, where it alighted and soon became a small, brown blur.

"Thank God, it seems all right!" the man said as he watched the bird fly away. "I'm sorry I didn't introduce myself properly. My name is Haitham; I'm here with my aunt, Nahed, who's visiting me from Egypt. Honestly, I thought I was going to be stuck in the office all weekend working on this big, boring engineering project, but she insisted I take her out for tea. I'm really glad I let her drag me out because it meant meeting someone as enchanting as yourself," he said with a grin.

Sawsan blushed.

"Interesting. So you're Egyptian? Your British accent's brilliant!" she said in amazement as she changed the topic.

Switching to Arabic, Sawsan continued: "I'm Lebanese, and it's so great to meet a fellow Arabic speaker! It's lovely to meet you, and it's wonderful that you're an animal lover."

Haitham answered back in his half-broken Egyptian accent as he hung his head shyly.

"You're too kind. It's nice meeting you too. If you're not too busy, would you like to join us on our table? My aunt looks like she's going to combust with curiosity," he said, gesturing to the colourfully dressed woman.

"I wouldn't want to impose…"

"Haitham! Ask that lovely creature to join us before I die of old age!" Nahed called out, gesturing to the empty chairs before her.

Haitham and Sawsan shared a quick laugh before joining her for a pleasant morning of crumpets and English breakfast tea.

The attraction was instantaneous, and after a whirlwind romance, they eventually got married in a quiet romantic ceremony, ignoring relatives' concerns about the scandalous fact that Sawsan was seven years older than her betrothed.

As Nahed concluded the story, she smiled down at the sleepy young lady, whose head lay on her lap. Stroking her hair tenderly, the elderly woman said: "Sleep now, angel."

Struggling to keep her eyes open, Allura smiled.

"What a wonderful story. It sounds like a fairy tale. Thanks for sharing it, Aunt Nahed," she said, yawning.

"With pleasure. Shush now, shut your eyes and try to sleep. You need it."

Nahed smiled as she watched Allura slip into deep sleep. She was happy to finally witness a peaceful smile on Allura's face. The older woman spent the whole night running her fingers through Allura's hair and recalling memories of Sawsan and Haitham, whom she missed deeply.

Chapter 6

Allura's New School

Months passed, and Allura began to adapt to life at her new school. She even made new friends from her swimming class. Allura retook to the water naturally, impressing her classmates and coach with her fitness and flair. The coach, spotting her talent, asked her to join the national swim team, which required extracurricular practice after school hours. She was flattered by the opportunity but knew that she'd have to work twice as hard, and wasn't sure the time was right, given that she only had one more year before graduating from school.

Outside the swimming pool, Allura didn't get along with her classmates very much. They represented a range of personalities, including the high-end spoilt brats, the low-key moderate crowd, punks, emos, hippies, preps, the overtly religious, the nerds and the gangsters. Each had their own characteristics, and she didn't fancy any of their lifestyles.

One of her classmates, who was particularly notorious, had bullied Allura since she arrived at the school. Jessy was a punk who had a huge crush on Bassel, Allura's closest friend and swim-mate. On a number of occasions, she'd attempted to stick gum in Allura's hair or scribble nasty comments on her locker. Allura never understood why Jessy acted that way around her and chose to keep as far away from her as possible. Jessy freaked her out.

Bassel was one of Egypt's top swimmers and always aced his grades. He was also very popular amongst the girls but never really took notice of them, since he was too absorbed with his swimming and studies.

He did, however, notice Allura. Their friendship was special; neither of them wanted to lose the closeness they felt towards one another, so they chose to turn what they shared and felt into a close friendship rather than a relationship. They were also close because of Bassel's international heritage – he had an Irish mother and Egyptian father – which reminded Allura of her cosmopolitan lifestyle back in Abu Dhabi.

Not a day passed by without Sawsan and Haitham crossing her mind, but Allura was determined to maintain happy and positive thoughts of her parents. She knew they were in a better place and focused all her thinking on trying to make them proud of her. She kept remembering her mother's words about how important it is to pursue an education she was passionate about and a career path she would enjoy.

In spite of not being a fan of her fellow pupils, Allura found several things she liked about her new school. Apart from swimming, she took an interest in English, literature, biology and technology classes and particularly enjoyed the art classes. She thought a lot about what steps she would take next after leaving school.

Both her swim coach and Bassel kept trying to persuade her to pursue professional swimming as a future. Bassel had already decided to study at the University of Michigan in the USA, through their athletic scholarship. He was keen on taking part in international swimming events and maybe even compete in the Olympics someday.

"You have a great future in swimming. Join me once you graduate from school and come study at Michigan," suggested Bassel as they dried themselves off from practice one afternoon. Their next classes weren't for another half an hour, so they always took the chance to talk before heading in separate directions.

"I love swimming, but I'm not crazy about it to the point that I'd take it up as a full-time career like you, Bassel. Besides, I want something more lasting. Professional swimmers peak so young. At best they last till their early thirties. You forget that you're only seventeen years old! Did you think of what it is you plan to do once you're too old to compete? You may be temporarily faster than anyone else, but our bodies age, and we eventually slow down."

"So what? Of course I've thought about it. But if I continue for long enough and with the way I envision it, by the time I reach my swimming retirement age, I'll be loaded," said Bassel with a chuckle. "Besides, there's always room to study something else. What's the big deal?"

"The big deal is that I don't see myself as working ten to fourteen hours a day, sometimes even more, in a swimming pool. I'm not like you. You're like a fish when you're in the pool. If you don't spend your whole day in the water, you get fidgety. I don't feel that way at all. I want to do something meaningful in my life. I want to be able to help people. I also love the idea of studying media relations or business. So, I'll see. Anyway, I've got a year left to make up my mind. I might even end up studying interior design. Did you know that UCLA has a strong interior design programme? I found out when I was looking at different universities yesterday. Maybe I'll apply for that and change my major if I don't like it – at least if I get in. And if I do, we'll both be in the States!"

Bassel smiled.

"Oh well, at least you're thinking of the States. The distance between California and Michigan by plane is about four hours, which isn't so bad. We can always visit one another. Allura, do you think we'd lose touch?"

"Who said we'd lose touch? Bassel, if I didn't know any better, I'd think this was a way for you to be with me."

"Of course I want to be with you!" replied Bassel, blushing darkly.

He was astonished at how fast he had connected with Allura. She spoke to him about anything that crossed her mind, including how she felt about her parents' passing. Her vulnerability made him grow fond of her.

"People don't have to know one another for a long time to get along. I know so many people who've spent time with each other for years, to discover later that they don't know each other at all. I also know people who have just met who feel instant chemistry and can talk to one another for hours about just anything," Allura mused.

"Are you seriously sixteen?"

"What do you mean?"

"It's like you're wise beyond your years, like you've got an old soul or something. You speak like an experienced woman, not a sixteen-year-old!"

"I've been through a lot and met many people in my life. My mum, rest her soul, always treated me like an adult. She constantly read to me when I was a little baby, and continued discussing the philosophy of life with me when I grew older. She taught me how to express myself, how to read between the lines, and how to take control of my own life."

Allura had only one concern, and that was leaving behind her aunt, whom she had grown close to already.

"You know what, Bassel? When my parents died in that accident, I felt that life was over for me. But after coming here, living with my aunt, and meeting you and the others, I know that there's a purpose and a meaning to all that's happened. I just don't know what it is right now."

"That's exactly what I admire about you, Allura. You choose to turn problems into opportunities. You deliberately chose a positive thought to dwell on, to keep your mind optimistic and your emotions intact."

As the bell rang, Bassel walked Allura to her classroom. "Take care, sunshine. Have a great class; I'll miss you," said Bassel.

Allura wasn't quite sure how to handle the shift appearing in their friendship. While curious to see how it would play out, the teenager was also apprehensive about ruining their special bond.

As she stepped into the classroom, Allura accidentally tripped over an outstretched foot. Righting herself, she groaned silently when she saw who it belonged to. It was Jessy.

Jessy had short, dyed hair and on most days wore black, skinny leather pants with leopard-print or patterned shirts that showed off her tattoos, bullet stud belts, band tees, and military-style boots. She had multiple facial and ear piercings and even a tongue stud.

"Daydreaming about lover boy, sunshine?" Jessy sneered. "Next time watch your step! Are you, like, blind or something?"

"Hey, that's not nice."

"Who the hell are you to speak to me about what's nice? You think you're anything close to nice? Stay in your own Little Miss Perfect World, you spoilt brat!"

Allura froze. She desperately wanted to walk away from Jessy's bullying but didn't want to show any signs of distress or weakness. She was afraid that things would escalate, especially since by that point Jessy had managed to attract the whole classroom's attention.

"You're such a lowlife loser, Jessy. I have no idea how people like you survive in this world," Allura yelled back.

"Oh you…!" Jessy pulled Allura's hair and raised her fist menacingly, but Allura was quicker. She slapped Jessy just as the biology teacher, Mrs Smith, walked into the classroom.

"Allura Mahmoud! What do you think you're doing? In the principal's office now!" said Mrs Smith in a stringent tone.

"Mrs Smith, it was Jessy who started. Ask anyone in the classroom. I was simply defending myself. She—"

"I said now!" the teacher interrupted sternly.

Allura waited by the principal's office until the bell rang, which was when Mrs Smith, accompanied by Jessy and Mohamed – whom everyone called Moe – caught up with her.

"Oh great, and what's he doing here? You bring a witness from class who just happens to be part of Jessy's funk punk gang. He's with her. He'll never tell the truth!"

"If I were you, Allura, I wouldn't utter a word right now. You're in serious trouble, and Moe volunteered to tell the truth about what exactly happened. If need be, we will ask the rest of your classmates too! Just stay put, and please do not utter a word till we all meet with the school principal. Is that clear?"

"Yes, Mrs Smith, it's clear. Sorry," said Allura apologetically.

The school principal, Mrs Roach, had known about Allura's situation before agreeing to enrol her at the school. If it hadn't been for Allura's high grades in her previous school, Mrs Roach wouldn't have allowed her to join the school during mid-year examinations. The principal was certain that Allura would easily catch up with the rest of her classmates. To further support her she had suggested to Nahed that Allura be offered extracurricular assistance if required, but it turned out to be unnecessary.

"Allura? I am surprised to see you in my office. Fancy meeting Jessy and Moe again, though. They visit me quite a lot. What's wrong now? What happened?" asked the middle-aged school principal.

"Well, Mrs Roach, I didn't witness the whole incident from the beginning, but as I was entering the classroom, I found Allura slapping Jessy. Moe has agreed to testify to what actually happened," said Mrs Smith.

"That's very strange behaviour coming out of you, Allura. Well, I'd like to hear what Moe has to say first, since he's volunteering to be a witness. Then, I'll hear from both Allura and Jessy. What happened, Moe? Start from the very beginning."

To Allura's astonishment, Moe told the entire truth about what occurred in the classroom.

"It looked like Jessy was bullying Allura. I mean, everyone knows Jessy has this huge crush on Bassel, so maybe she was jealous or something," Moe explained.

"Moe, you two-faced brat! You skunk, you call yourself my friend? Oh, you little—" Jessy was infuriated.

"Young lady! You put your voice down this instant! Learn to control your temper and respect yourself. May I remind you that you are in my office and under serious interrogation! This is not the first time you've gotten yourself into serious trouble. Do you know the severe mess you may have just put yourself into? You could be suspended today, so if I were you I would sit in silence and speak very little, if at all, unless asked. Do you understand what I'm saying, Jessy?"

"Yes, Mrs Roach. I'm sorry," answered Jessy sulkily, rolling her eyes.

Mrs Roach decided to speak to a few more pupils who had witnessed the incident. They all reaffirmed what Moe had described earlier.

Jessy was instantly suspended for the rest of the year due to similar bullying behaviour in the past that she had been warned not to repeat.

Allura wasn't sure where her fate lay. She prayed that she too wouldn't be dismissed or suspended as she waited impatiently for the interrogation to end.

When Mrs Roach was ready to speak with Allura she asked Mrs Smith, Moe and the rest of the pupils to leave the room.

"Allura, please stay behind. I need to talk to you for a few minutes," said Mrs Roach, as she invited her to sit on a cool leather couch conveniently located in front of her office desk.

"Sure, Mrs Roach." Allura prayed she wasn't in trouble.

"How are you?"

"How do you mean?"

"I mean, life at school can be stressful. How are you coping, given that—"

"Given that I've just lost both my parents? I'm fine, I guess! Things are a bit different here, and I don't have as many friends as I used to in my previous school, but I'm getting by."

"Well, I'll always be here if you ever need to talk to someone."

"Do I look like I need support, Mrs Roach?"

"I'm just making sure you're all right, Allura. Don't be offended. I have no complaints regarding your academic progress. Your grades are great! What are your plans for next year? Have you thought of which college you'd like to go to once you're done with high school?"

"I thought of UCLA."

"Interesting, and why that particular university?"

"Well, for starters, my dad has a condo near the college campus. Secondly, they have interior design as a major, which I've always been passionate about. Plus, if I get bored with that, I can always switch to something else."

"What makes you feel you'll get bored of interior design?"

"I don't know. Everyone says that interior design isn't really a proper major or career. I guess I'll find out when I get there."

"Well, what do you like most about interior designing?"

"I read that to be an interior designer you need to be skilled in both architecture and decoration. You need to be able to work with the vision of the person who hired you, yet add your own personal flair. You have to think of minute details, including the size of the room, suitable colours and the style your client has in mind. It's just so creative!"

"It seems to me that this is something you're very passionate about, and obviously you've read up on the subject."

Mrs Roach was impressed that for a subject Allura claimed to be unsure about, the excited pupil in front of her already seemed rather knowledgeable about that field. Even if subconsciously, it seemed that Allura had already set her mind to what it was she'd like to do in the future.

By the time their conversation had ended, so had the school day. As Allura walked out of Mrs Roach's office, she was relieved that Jessy got what she deserved, and that she hadn't been punished.

"Thanks for your time, Mrs Roach. Am I off the hook?"

"Yes, just this time. Just don't slap anyone again – or get physical at all for that matter, even if you're defending yourself. Otherwise, I will have to take serious action. Please don't let peer pressure change the beautiful person you are. Take care of yourself, and remember, my door is always open."

Chapter 7

Friday Night Fever

The weekend had finally arrived, and Allura and several friends from her swimming class were taking full advantage of the free time that stretched before them, starting with watching a movie at the mall. As they walked out of the theatre, Allura spotted Jessy and her notorious gang of punks emerging from a different movie.

"Oh, no!" groaned Allura.

"What is it?" asked Dania.

"It's Jessy! I really don't want to spoil my Friday night. Oh God, please, no!" she complained in fright.

The group exchanged uneasy glances. Everyone had heard what had happened between Allura and Jessy a few days ago. Jessy had tried her best to spread rumours about how Allura had pull with the principal, which resulted in Jessy's suspension.

"Is there any back door or any other entrance? I need to avoid that maniac. I won't let her spoil my Friday night," Allura asked anxiously.

"No, it looks like there's only one entrance and exit," replied Nancy as she craned her neck to look for another way out. The girls could see Jessy and her gang crowding the doorway, smoking cigarettes and chatting.

"Should we go back in and grab a bite to eat till those losers decide to leave?" suggested Dania.

"That's a great idea, but my aunt will freak out if I arrive later than ten," said Allura.

"Well, then call her!" advised Tia.

Sighing deeply, Allura called her aunt. She had been looking forward to a fun night out, but it seemed that it was on the verge of being ruined.

"Hi, auntie. I'm just letting you know that I'm still with my friends, but we're thinking of having dinner before we leave. Is that OK?"

"That's fine; just make sure you get home by curfew. It's already after nine, dear," answered Nahed.

Nahed chose to trust Allura. She was confident that Sawsan and Haitham had done a good job in bringing their daughter up properly, yet she worried about the type of people Allura hung out with. She knew how tempting things could get in a big city like Cairo, which was known to get wild at night. She was concerned that Allura would get mixed up with the wrong type of crowd.

"Well, we're about to go and grab something to eat now. How about I call you the minute I'm ready to leave the mall?"

"Fine, Allura, but please do take care of yourself. You mentioned that one of your friends has a car. Are you sure she'll drop you off safely? Is she a good driver?"

"Yes, Tia is a great driver, and she lives close to our place. She'll drop me. Don't worry, Auntie Nahed."

"All right, Allura. Take good care of yourself. See you soon."

The girls headed off to a nearby café, where they enjoyed chocolate pancakes and laughed off the situation. Despite Allura's distress, her friends did all they could to keep her occupied. They spoke about the movie they had just watched, and discussed some of the funniest scenes that had made them laugh.

An hour later, they paid the bill and exchanged goodbyes. On their way out of the mall, Tia and Allura detoured to the nearest ladies' room to freshen up before leaving. As they approached the bathroom, Allura's heart dropped.

"Tia, it's Moe! Oh man, it's just not my night. They're still here," sighed Allura.

"Moe who?"

"Moe, Tia! Jessy's friend, the guy who volunteered to speak to the school principal about the whole incident, remember?"

"Oh, him. But hey, you mentioned that he was on your side. I mean, he was supportive, right? So what's the problem?"

"He's still her friend, and he's out with her tonight, isn't he? That means she might not be far behind."

"You're starting to freak me out. I can call my older brother to meet us, in case things get nasty. I think he's nearby somewhere with his friends."

Allura's hands were trembling. She had just about enough from Jessy and her group and had gone through a tough year already. She wasn't about to tolerate any more anxiety in her life.

"Look who's here. Hey, Allura, how you doing?" Moe said, smirking.

"Haven't I seen you in school?" he said, turning to Tia in curiosity. "You're in the twelfth grade, right?"

Tia nodded. "Yeah, hi. I'm Tia."

"Well, hello there, Tia. Pleasure to meet you. So what are you two beautiful dames doing on a Friday night in this part of town?" Moe wasn't your typical punk, though he hung out with them. He looked the part too, with baggy jeans, torn sneakers and a graphic t-shirt. His hair was in a faux-hawk, and he had a brow ring piercing.

"Are you with Jessy and the rest of the group?" asked Allura. It was all she could think about.

"Yeah, we were watching a movie. How about you? What are you doing here?"

"Same thing, watching a movie."

Tia was standing there looking at the two of them thinking how awkward the situation was. Moe didn't scare her; his friends were the real problem. She definitely related to how Allura felt and decided to cut the conversation short.

"Moe, sorry to interrupt you, but we're about to head home. It was nice meeting you. See you around sometime?"

Just as Tia was about to tug Allura away, her friend suddenly blurted: "Moe, I didn't really get the chance to thank you earlier for standing by me during the interrogation at the principal's office, and I need to ask you for a favour."

Tia rolled her eyes. She didn't quite understand why Allura was still continuing her conversation with a supposedly troubled teen.

"Sure, Allura. What's up?"

"Well, in all honesty, Jessy freaks the living hell out of me. I mean she's absolutely insane, and I know she can't stand me either. I don't want any more problems. Can you possibly distract her so we can leave the mall in peace?"

Moe laughed. "Jessy isn't that scary, you know."

"She is to me, Moe. I really don't want to get caught in an uncomfortable situation right now."

"Allura, Jessy's bark is worse than her bite. She's just got a loud mouth on her. That's about it," replied Moe.

"Well, I honestly don't care to know anything about what Jessy is like. I just need to get the hell out of this mall in one piece, and I'm asking you to help. Will you help or not?"

"Chill, geez. Relax, woman! No worries, I'll help. Just give me ten minutes."

Moe turned away before stopping. Glancing back, he asked: "Do you happen to have a boyfriend, by the way? Are you dating that Bassel dude?"

"Huh? No, I don't have a boyfriend, and no, I am not dating Bassel. We're just really good friends. Now could you please focus on distracting your friends till we rush out of the mall?"

"Sure, stay put till I phone you. Speaking of which, can I have your phone number?"

Moe couldn't believe his luck. This was the perfect opportunity to strike and get the number of the girl of his dreams.

"Of course you can't have my phone number!"

"Fine then, stay here all night!"

As he walked away, Allura called out: "Moe, Moe, wait! Here, here's my number. Give me a missed call the second you manage to get them out of here."

"Okie dokie!" Moe said, sauntering away with a skip in his step.

"Why on earth did you just do that? How can you give him your phone number?" Tia questioned in stark disbelief.

"What choice did I have?"

"You could have asked him to come back and find us. He'd even help accompany us to the car!"

"That would have taken far too long, and I'm already late. My aunt doesn't go to sleep before I get home. I just won't answer his phone calls if he ever tries to contact me."

Allura and Tia waited impatiently. True to his word, Moe gave a missed call ten minutes later, and they rushed towards the exit. Arriving safely to the car, the girls gave a sigh of relief. To be on the safe side, Tia locked the doors before turning on the engine.

"No!" Allura shouted.

"What is it, Allura?" Tia was startled. She thought Jessy had suddenly appeared out of nowhere. "Is she here? What is it?"

"Don't lock those doors!"

"Damn it, Allura, what is wrong with you tonight? You startled me! I thought those punks were about to attack us or something. Chill out, will you? Fine, I won't lock the doors. To be honest, it's just a habit. I feel safe when I lock my car doors!"

"Not around me, Tia. Don't lock your car doors around me, please! Otherwise I'll just walk home."

"Sheesh, fine, I won't lock the doors. Can you please just relax now? You're all worked up tonight."

Tia knew about Allura's parents, but had no idea why she had freaked out about locking the car doors. In any case, it was a conversation for another day. Right now, Tia's priority was getting her friend home before she got into trouble.

"OK, well, the good news is that we're safe now. We're out of here!" said Tia with a smirk on her face as she drove past the mall.

"Yeah, but for how long? Those guys are weird. Jessy scares me, and I know she'll keep harassing me till she gets back at me in her own evil way!"

"Nah, I have to agree with Moe on this one. Jessy just dresses all funny and uses foul language to back up her weird voodoo style, nothing more. Actually, I kind of feel sorry for her. She's probably an insecure and lonely person deep down inside."

"You think so? Why do you say that?"

"Oh, I know so! People like that have had it bad; I bet she's had an unpleasant past. She doesn't know any better, I guess."

"Well, I've had a rough past. You don't see me treating people that way. She's wild and out of control. If you're trying to make me feel sorry for her, it's not working."

"That's not what I meant, silly. I mean she's probably been bullied or abused herself. Behind all that aggression is hidden anger. I pity people like that; they hardly have anything to look forward to in life."

"I still don't feel sorry for her. There's no excuse for her crazy behaviour. But you know what? You should actually take up psychology. You seem to enjoy analysing people."

Tia laughed. "Maybe I will. Who knows? For now, I'm just glad that we got out of there in one piece. After meeting Moe, I kind of feel ridiculous for getting worked up about them."

"I have the exact same feeling; I'm just relieved we got out of there safely."

By the time Allura arrived home, her fear was replaced by irritation. Jessy had ruined her night out and worked her up to the point of nearly having a panic attack. As she locked the front door behind her, Allura hoped that would be the last time she'd ever have to see Jessy again.

Chapter 8

New Lessons Learnt

Weeks had passed since the mall incident. Allura had forgotten all about what happened as she focused on her end-of-year examinations. She even began skipping her swimming classes to make sure that her full concentration was on her studies. She and Bassel weren't seeing one another as much as they used to; he was busy focusing on getting everything together for his university applications.

Eager to make use of her spare time once the school year was over, Allura decided to look around for some summer jobs. She had already spoken with her aunt about the possibility, and Nahed had promised to ask her acquaintances for any potential opportunities.

Flavio and Lucy, who were regularly in touch with Allura and Nahed, had invited Allura to visit them in Abu Dhabi for the summer break; she declined the offer politely, not ready to go back just yet.

"Allura, you're still in school, and you just turned seventeen. You need to lower your expectations a bit and accept what's out there," advised Nahed.

"So I basically don't have a choice about where I work during the summer?"

"Well, it would be great if you could land your dream job right now, but things don't come that easy. I'll ask around to see if there's anything in interior design, but you have to be flexible in case something else comes along. Also, keep in mind that as a high school student, you'll either be working for free or for very little money."

"That's fine. I'll take anything, just as long as I gain experience. I really want to make Mum and Dad proud of me."

"Honey, rest assured, your mum and dad are already proud of you, as I am."

After speaking to a few of her friends and pulling a few strings, Nahed landed a job for Allura as an administrative secretary at a medical centre for the elderly, which was located close to where they lived. She'd be in charge of filing, typing, answering the phone and assisting staff when needed. The job didn't sound too interesting for Allura, but she agreed to take it. At least, she would earn little spending money during her two and a half months at the centre.

A month passed, and Allura started her new job at the centre. It was beautiful, with a huge, colourful front yard that had all types of flowers imaginable. Allura loved taking breaks just to sit and admire the blooms. She was given a typical shift, which meant working about fifty hours a week, with weekends off. She quickly found the job to be repetitive and dull, which is when she decided to check whether there was an opening in another department.

As Allura walked into the Human Resources department, she noticed a young male receptionist who seemed to be dwarfed by piles of paperwork. Looking his way, she greeted him with a smile. "Good morning. Is there someone I can speak to regarding my job here in the centre? I was wondering if there was a new project I could work on, or maybe even a new department I could join?"

The man waved his hand vaguely to the right, still absorbed with the papers in front of him. "Speak to that woman back there."

Allura frowned. She felt offended at how impolite and incompetent the receptionist seemed.

"Excuse me? Can you kindly look my way? I was courteous with you and expect the same in return. How have you been employed as a receptionist if you can't do your job properly? Don't you know that the number one rule in any organisation is proper communication skills?"

Ahmed was startled. He wasn't expecting such a response from a little slip of a girl who probably only got the job because it was something that would look good on her university applications.

"You're right," he said. "I'm sorry; you just caught me at a bad time. I'm busy working on some pending hospital bills. If I make a mistake with these, it could mean my neck."

"Well, now that you explain yourself, I can understand. You could have just said that from the beginning, I won't keep you then. I'll go speak to her," she said, nodding towards the heavyset woman in the corner.

"No! I mean, no, it's OK. I needed to take a break anyway. How can I help you? Oh, sorry, I'm Ahmed by the way," he said, reaching out to shake her hand.

As he looked up to face her, to her utter mortification, Allura began to blush. Sitting down in front of the attractive, tanned man, she took a deep breath and prayed she wouldn't stammer or embarrass herself further.

"How about we start over? Now how is it I can help you again?"

Ahmed was charming. He had mysterious, hazel eyes and a genuine smile. When he stood up to apologise, he was well over six feet tall, which impressed her; she loved tall men. In her eyes, he was very masculine and seemed committed to his job. He looked like he was in his mid-twenties.

Allura felt very bad about initially speaking to him that way and remembered her mother's words about thinking about her words before deciding to open her little trap.

"I just wanted to meet with someone about my job responsibilities," she said, in a calmer tone. A shy smile lit her face.

"I could probably help, then, if you don't mind speaking to a man," replied Ahmed.

Allura's face reddened. "Of course I don't, that wouldn't bother me at all, on the contrary," she stuttered, as she self-consciously bit her lip. She folded her hands in her lap as she gathered her thoughts.

"Well, I've been training here for just over three weeks as an administrative secretary in Ward B on the second floor. I file, type and answer phone calls, but it's pretty boring. Filing doesn't take ten minutes of my time, and answering phone calls is just not my thing at all. I feel I have more to offer, to be honest. This is my first job, and I'd really like to learn something new and challenging. Are there any other opportunities for me at the centre?"

"Hmmm, what's your name again?"

"Allura Mahmoud. I'm the new trainee here."

"Right. Well, Allura Mahmoud, you've been in this centre for almost a month now. What is it that interests you the most about this place?"

"Honestly, nothing! It's so morbid here – but please don't tell anyone I just said that. I don't want to offend anyone!"

Ahmed was charmed by the innocent woman – no, teenage girl, he reminded himself – before him. It was obvious that Allura had no work experience or even life experience. He found himself being drawn into a desire to help her and possibly get to know her better.

"Is this your first work experience?"

"Yes, it is. I'm really disappointed, to be honest. It is not how I envisioned a first job to be."

"How old are you, if I may ask?"

"I just turned seventeen, old enough!"

Ahmed laughed. "Allura, you've got audacity!"

"Thanks, I guess, I'll assume that's a good thing?" she responded as she stared at the floor, blushing.

"Well, you're very young. Don't you think you're being too judgemental and hasty, given the fact that this is your first job, ever?"

"Well, that's exactly why I'm here talking to you. I want to enjoy what I do and also make some sort of contribution while I'm here, to learn and gain experience. I need to put something on my application forms other than the fact that I type, file and try to look busy and pretty all day with a phone stuck to my ear."

Ahmed respected Allura's honesty and decided to help her discover her potential, or at least some hidden skills, while she was at the centre. He was also worried that she'd get too bored and decide to leave.

"OK, tell you what. How about you spend today with me? I'll give you a proper tour of the place and introduce you to the staff and patients. It would be nice for them to see a new face. You could always volunteer to help with other things around here if you think your day's too quiet."

"Oh yes, that sounds so much more interesting. Thank you!"

"My pleasure. Just give me an hour to finish up here and I'll come find you. Ward B on the second floor, am I right?"

"Yes, that's right, the last room at the end of the corridor to the right."

As Allura walked back to her ward, Josephine, the head nurse, raised a quizzical eyebrow at the young woman's flushed face and broad smile.

"I haven't seen you smile like this since you joined us. What's got you so happy today?" she asked in curiosity.

"Oh, nothing. Just met the dreamiest guy ever. His name's Ahmed, and he works in HR, I think. Have you seen him? His eyes are so gorgeous. Oh!" Allura abruptly stopped her ramblings. Groaning in embarrassment, she hid her face in her hands. "Is there a chance you could forget what I just mumbled?"

Josephine giggled. "The HR receptionist happens to be a woman. Can you describe him to me?"

"Oh. Um, he's tall, with black hair and hazel eyes. I think he's in his twenties."

"Do you mean Dr Ahmed Barakat! He's the son of the centre's owner and chief medical officer, Dr Shawki Barakat. He was probably sitting at the reception area to review something, and you happened to be passing by. Allura, you crack me up!"

"You're joking! I need to dig a hole in this ground right here, right now and dive inside and never come out. I actually yelled at him and called him rude! He said he was going to meet me here in an hour! What am I supposed to do? Oh God, this is beyond embarrassing.”

“Nothing, just act like you never heard anything!”

“How can I do that? Now that you told me, I can’t possibly look him in the face again.”

Josephine smiled. Allura definitely needed to learn a thing or two about life.

“Then, don’t. Just look down!” said Josephine with a laugh. “Come on, it’s not that bad!”

“It is that bad!” Allura felt very embarrassed by the whole situation.

Ahmed had joined the centre as a geriatric psychiatrist after graduating from medical school, and soon found himself being given senior responsibilities to help oversee the centre with his father. It was something he found he rather enjoyed, especially when he got to organise various recreational activities for the staff and patients. It did take a toll on his social life though, not that he’d noticed.

Looking up from his desk, Ahmed quickly stood up. It was time to meet Allura. He hadn’t felt this excited about anything in a very long time. He had to sternly remind himself that she was a child, a teenager.

Nodding his head at everyone who greeted him, Ahmed soon found himself practically jogging to Ward B. He broke out into a wide smile when he saw Allura.

“Hello again, Allura. Are you ready for the grand tour?”

“Hello, Dr Ahmed. Yes, I am, and I want to apologise for my behaviour earlier. I had no right to speak to you like that,” she said, twisting her hands.

“Oh darn, who spilled the beans? Anyway, it’s Ahmed, and don’t worry about it. I’m actually glad you spoke to me that way; it broke me out of my zombie zone and showed that you’ve got passion, which is good. It’s something that will take you far in life. Now, let’s go on that tour.”

Allura was surprised by his response and sped up her pace to keep up with his long strides.

He started the tour with the top floor. “So this is where all the big people work,” said Ahmed with a smile. “The chief medical officer, the chief financial officer and all the rest of the management team are here. The staff calls it the Floor to Avoid."

"And your office is here, of course. You are considered management too, right?" asked Allura.

"Well no, my office isn't here; it's closer to my patients." Seeing her confusion, he continued: "It's just easier that way, since I can quickly check up on them. Hold on for a sec."

Stopping at a door labelled 'Supplies', Ahmed reached in and grabbed a white robe and stethoscope.

"What type of patients do you have?" asked Allura.

"I mostly deal with elderly patients who have different illnesses, like Alzheimer's disease or senile dementia. Do you know what those are?"

"Well, they forget things or need assistance with tasks, like getting dressed, right?"

"Exactly, that's right. Some of the other conditions among patients rehabilitated here include fractured femurs, knee and hip replacement, Parkinson's disease and strokes."

"You see each and every single one of these patients? What do you do, exactly?"

"Well, I'm a geropsychiatrist, which is a sub-specialty of psychiatry. I deal with the prevention and treatment of psychological and mental disorders among elderly people."

"That sounds complicated."

Ahmed roared with laughter. "It's not so bad. I studied geriatric medicine for seven years."

"Wow, seven whole years? That's a very long time! Congratulations! You're done, though. I still haven't even entered university yet," said Allura with a sigh.

"Ha-ha, done? I wish!"

"What do you mean? Didn't you say you studied for seven years? Did you fail or something?"

Ahmed laughed at how naive Allura's questions were but found them rather intriguing.

"Allura, it takes around seven years to study medicine, and it doesn't end there. I'm now in the process of completing my four-year residency in psychiatry and a one-year fellowship in geriatric psychiatry."

"Oh my God, that's twelve years of studying! And here I am thinking that school takes too long! I cannot imagine studying a total of twenty-four years! You'll be ancient by the time you graduate!"

Ahmed skidded to a stop. "How old do you think I am?"

"I dunno, twenty-eight? Thirty?"

"I'm twenty-six years old," he replied in amusement.

Allura gasped. "No way!"

"Yup, so I'll probably be in my mid-thirties by the time I'm done. Not too young, but not ancient either."

Allura covered her face for the umpteenth time. "I'm so embarrassed. I should just keep my mouth shut!"

Ahmed chuckled. "Don't worry about it. I tell you what, let's forget that conversation ever happened. Now, let's continue with our tour."

Allura hadn't been given a proper orientation to the centre before and hadn't met with any of the patients. As they cruised the building, Dr Ahmed pointed out the custom-made facilities and infrastructure that had been specially designed to assist patients with Alzheimer's and dementia. The colour-coded wards helped patients identify where they were, while the motion-activated lights were installed to help them navigate the ward at night. The flooring consisted of plain mats in order to avoid unnecessary falls or accidents.

Each ward contained a huge nursing reception area that was accessible to all the rooms. There was a sensory area that had calm music and a soothing aroma to help patients relax. The centre was also equipped with a gymnasium, a social centre that consisted of a mini-cinema and various recreational games and activities, and a cafeteria that offered healthy snacks and food.

After touring the centre with Dr Ahmed, Allura regretted calling it morbid and depressing. She resolved to never judge anything or anyone again without first having all the facts. Allura was even given the chance to speak to several patients. She particularly enjoyed speaking with Sherif Sarwat, a seventy-six-year-old French-Egyptian who suffered from Alzheimer's. He was a jolly fellow who happened to be one of Dr Ahmed's favourite patients too.

As they walked back to Ward B, Allura asked Ahmed once again what she could do to help the centre other than just being an administrative secretary. He was impressed by her enthusiasm and suggested that she come up with new recreational ideas. Allura zealously agreed to take on the task.

To familiarise herself with the current programme, Ahmed suggested that she visit his office and take a look at what had already been planned. Nodding in agreement, Allura seemed practically ready to grab his hand and drag him there. Ahmed was secretly disappointed that she didn't, and it took all of his willpower to bid her goodbye and go back to his rounds with Allura's gaze burning into his back.

Chapter 9

The Park

It was a beautiful early Monday morning, the kind that could only be described as picture perfect, with white, fluffy clouds and a gentle breeze. The fresh air in that part of town, especially with all the greenery around, was simply rejuvenating. It had taken nearly a month to organise the trip to one of Cairo's most celebrated public parks after Allura submitted a detailed proposal to the centre's top management.

The group of fifteen patients assisted by eight nurses, five assistant nurses and Dr Ahmed settled down in the area Allura had picked out earlier, which was already equipped with a mattress, a plastic table and matching chairs, and folding beach loungers. Allura had even gotten permission from her aunt to borrow her chef for the day to make sure that everything was as perfect as possible.

The highlight of the whole event was a young band that played music from the fifties and sixties. Soon the patients were happily eating and socialising as they enjoyed the beautiful atmosphere around them. Some played cards, and others took strolls around the park with the help of an assistant.

Allura was busy running around, making sure everything was in place when Ahmed called out to her from his lounge chair: "Take a breather, Allura. Sit down for a while. You must be exhausted!"

"I'm all right. I've all this energy, and I want to make sure everything's all right. Are you having fun, Ahmed?"

Allura was the only person at the centre allowed to call him Ahmed, other than his father. She appreciated the way he treated her differently from the rest of the employees at the centre. Her admiration quickly turned to attraction, but she tried her best to hide it. He was a proper adult, and she was still a teenager. He was good to her and taught her a lot. She didn't want to jeopardise whatever their relationship was.

"Look around you. Look at what you've accomplished. All the patients are smiling. Even the nurses and staff are having a brilliant time. Look at Nurse Josephine, the most uptight person I know. She's even taken off her shoes!" Ahmed smiled, gesturing to the middle-aged woman.

Ahmed was surprised that she had managed to organise everything so efficiently and in such a short span of time. He liked her motivation and perseverance and felt happy to be in her presence. She was definitely a breath of fresh air for everyone. His life was monotonous, he had forgotten about how pleasant life could be at times.

Allura laughed. "So does that mean you'll allow me to organise another trip and different activities for the rest of the patients at the centre?"

"Sure! You're a natural at it, and you seem to enjoy making people happy."

"That's true. I love seeing smiles on people's faces, and I grew attached to the patients at the centre, especially Sherif. He's become my mentor."

"Well, you're welcome to stay at the centre for as long as you want. At least until summer ends. Then you have to go back to school, right?"

"Yeah, it's my final year of high school. I can't wait. Maybe, after I graduate from university, I can come back and work here full time, if that's all right with you," said Allura.

"Of course that's all right with me. It would be a pleasure. But is that what you want to do with your life? You strike me as being more of an artistic person. What do you want to do with your life, Allura?"

"I really don't know anymore. I had plans to travel to California and study interior design. I'm also interested in other things, and after working at the centre, I realised that I also love working with people and organising events. It's so confusing!"

"Well, I'm sure you'll find your way. You're a bright, young girl. You'll figure it out."

"How did you end up being a doctor? I mean, did you know that this was what you wanted to be?"

"Yes, since I was a child. My father and our whole family are doctors, and it's all I ever knew growing up."

"But you seem to enjoy it. I mean, it was also a decision of yours to become a doctor, right?"

"Like I said, it's all I ever knew, which makes it a duty more than just a decision."

Allura wasn't sure how to respond. Ahmed noticed her discomfort and changed the subject.

"So you've warmed up to Sherif at the centre, huh? Look at him now, he's clearly enjoying the food. Your aunt's chef must have at least one Michelin star!"

Allura just then noticed that Ahmed wasn't eating. "How come you haven't tried the food? Aren't you hungry?"

"I'm a vegetarian; I don't eat meat or chicken."

"But there's plenty of vegetables and fruits, and a huge bowl of salad. Do you want me to get you a plate?"

"Don't worry about me. I'm enjoying the weather and relaxing for now. I'll grab a plate later."

Just then, Bassel's name appeared on her mobile phone. Allura hesitated. She missed speaking to him. But at the same time, she'd finally managed to have a personal conversation with Ahmed, and she didn't want to ruin her opportunity to get to know him better. Before she could change her mind, she accepted the call.

"Would you excuse me for just a few minutes, Ahmed? I have to take this call."

"By all means. Please, take your time."

Allura got up and started to walk away, looking for somewhere slightly more private to speak to Bassel.

"Hello, Allura. How have you been?"

"Bassel, how are you? I've missed you. Where've you been all this time?"

"I should ask you the same thing. You disappeared on me. I tried to phone you a few times, but you never pick up when I call."

"I'm sorry, Bassel. I started a new summer job, and I've been very busy. When are you travelling to Michigan? I can't believe how time flies, and that you're actually leaving to university already!"

"I leave tonight. New job? Wow, that's great news. What do you do?"

"Did you just say tonight? Are you serious? And you call me on your very last day?"

"Yes, my flight takes off at eleven tonight. It's almost a fifteen-hour flight. Can you believe it? I'll land at around two in the afternoon, US time. I'm really not looking forward to the jet lag. I'll miss you, Allura. I'll write to you. I have your personal e-mail address, and of course we always have chat."

"Is there any way we can meet before you travel? I really want to say goodbye to you in person!"

"I was never very good with goodbyes, so let's try to avoid that. You never answered my question. What do you do in that new summer job?"

"Well, that's a pretty interesting story. I started off as a secretary, and now I'm working as an events coordinator at a medical centre for the elderly."

"A centre for the elderly?" Bassel laughed. "You're full of surprises, Allura! Well, good luck. I've always been very impressed by your dedication. Keep it up, and we'll catch up properly soon. Take care. I'll miss you."

"I'll miss you too, Bassel, and I'm sure I'll hear brilliant news about your swimming achievements. I can't wait to hear about how life treats you in Michigan."

"I promise I'll stay in touch, but you need to do the same too! I don't want to find out everything through social media or our friends, OK?"

"Sure. I promise. You know you're very dear to me."

"Ditto. Oh, one more thing before you hang up. This is your last year. Make it count. Make sure you surround yourself with the right kind of people, OK?"

"What do you mean?"

"I mean, don't just hang out with people because you'd like to fit in. Choose your friends. Cairo is a huge city, and there are so many different types of people out there. Just take care whom you befriend, whom you talk to, and whom you choose to spend most of your time with. You're a genuine character and very attractive from all perspectives; I don't want anything or anyone to end up hurting you."

"Don't worry, I'm a big girl. I'll be fine. You just take good care of yourself."

Once they hung up, Allura went back to where the group of patients were gathered. She was slightly disheartened after the phone call. Now that Bassel was gone, she wasn't sure she'd meet anyone quite like him again. She reminded herself that what they shared was stronger than the distance between them and that they'd stay in touch. Bassel was wise and trustworthy, and she wasn't about to give up on a person with these traits just because of the distance.

"Welcome back, Allura. It's a beautiful day out. I say we take advantage of this splendid weather. Care to make an old man happy and join me for a walk across this beautiful park?" It was Allura's favourite patient, Sherif, who had noticed her sad expression.

"Sure, why not? With pleasure, Bassel."

"Bassel?"

"Oh, I'm so sorry. I meant Sherif! I was just talking to my best friend, Bassel. He's travelling tonight to the USA. I won't see him in quite some time, so I'm a bit pre-occupied about that thought, sorry."

As they walked down a long lane bordered by colourful flowers, Allura assisted Sherif by placing her arms around him.

Sherif paused for a second. "My sweet child, you are an angel. Look at your face, full of purity. Yet you seem so unhappy."

"You're just too kind, Sherif. But yeah, you're right about the unhappy part."

"So tell me, what's bothering you, child?"

"Like I just said, one of my best friends is travelling tonight to Michigan. It's just that—" She hesitated a bit. "Well, I'm going to miss having him around. I'm not very good with goodbyes."

"C'est la vie, cherie. You need to get used to exchanging goodbyes. It's what life is all about. After newborns arrive to the world, some depart too early. Some stay till they're older, like your old man here, and others travel to a new destination. It's the reason why we exist, to come and go. It's a short journey that seems long at times but ends faster than you expect it to."

"Do you feel your journey is ending fast, Sherif?"

"Too fast, my dear. Which is exactly why one should embrace life. Enjoy your health, your youth, your friends and your family. Enjoy breathing, Allura, for as long as you have health, you are blessed."

"Yes, you're right, Sherif. Speaking about taking advantage of the moment – or moments, for that matter," said Allura, smiling. "I was wondering if it would be all right to ask you something about Dr Ahmed?"

Sherif nodded his head. He wasn't quite sure what Allura was referring to but remained attentive to what she was saying. "Yes, child, you can speak to me about anything you want."

"Do you think I'm stupid to have a massive crush on Dr Ahmed?" Allura was comfortable sharing her secrets with Sherif since she trusted his wisdom and advice. As bad as it felt, it was reassuring to know that he'd forget about their conversation eventually anyway.

"One should never call oneself stupid when it comes to feelings. On the contrary, enjoy how you feel about him. Why are you blaming yourself for feeling this way?"

"Well, for one, it's unprofessional. He's the owner's son and a reputable doctor who's eight years older than me. I'm not even in his league; he'd never look at a child like me."

"Don't underestimate yourself. You're a charming, young lady. I'm sure he does fancy you, but in his own way."

Sherif had a pleasant face; he spoke his words with a warm smile and sincerity. He had developed Alzheimer's a year ago, and it was getting worse by the day. He was still in the mid-stages of the disease, so at times he had some sort of recall of certain things. His selective memory was based on how much things meant to him.

"How do you know that, Sherif? Did he tell you?"

"Did who tell me what?"

"Dr Ahmed. Did he tell you that he fancies me?"

"Did I just say that?"

"Yes, just now. You said he fancied me!"

"I didn't say that!"

Allura sighed in frustration. Sherif's Alzheimer's had struck again. At the same time though, she couldn't stop thinking of that small blossom of hope that he had planted in her heart. *Could that be even halfway true? Did Dr Ahmed really like her back?*

She decided to disregard the thought. It couldn't possibly have been true, and Sherif probably had no idea about what he was talking about.

Glancing at her watch, Allura noticed that it was time to head back. Grasping Sherif's arm firmly, she guided him back to the group, where she managed the dismantling of everything and made sure everyone was safely on the bus back to the centre.

Chapter 10

Surprise Visit

It was Allura's final week at the centre, something that filled her with bittersweet joy. She was delighted to have met so many interesting people and learnt a few things along the way, but now it was time to go back to reality and focus on her last year at school.

During her time there, Allura realised that she didn't want to work as an interior designer anymore. She spoke to her aunt, friends and even Ahmed about what other fields and universities she could consider. Allura knew she wanted to do something that would make her parents proud but also satisfy her passion. Finally, she decided to pick out a practical major: business administration.

She had never been big on reporting to people for too long anyway. She felt that the only logical thing to do after gaining relevant experience, was to open her own business.

She knew her parents had made sure she'd never want for anything and vowed to use her inheritance wisely, while also making sure that she'd be helping other people.

It was noon on a Sunday when Allura received a call from Ahmed asking her to meet him in Ward A, in the room of a mid-sixties patient called Fatima. The doctor's clipped tone made Allura anxious as she hurried to the specified room. To her surprise, she found Moe sitting on a side chair next to Fatima's bed.

"Moe? What's going on? What are you doing here?" she asked in surprise.

"I should ask you the same thing," said Moe suspiciously. Allura hardly recognised him: he had shaved his hair and removed all his piercings. He wore a neatly ironed white shirt, dark blue jeans, and regular walking shoes.

"I work here as an intern. I still have one more week to go. How about you? This is such a surprise!"

"Well, I'm here visiting my grandmother, Nana Fatima."

Dr Ahmed intervened. "Fatima is one of my patients, Allura. I was checking up on her when her grandson happened to be here. We briefly talked, and when I asked him which school he attended, I found out that you two were in the same classroom last year. It's a small world! So I decided to call you in, since you're apparently good friends."

"Well, I'm not sure about being good friends," said Allura. "But yeah, I know Moe. So what's new? You've cleaned up since I last saw you!"

Moe cleared his throat portentously. "Well, I have to look different. I'm here visiting my grandmother. You gotta look all sharp and clean for Grannie, right?"

"Well, that's nice. It's a funny coincidence. How about I show you around, if you'd like?" Allura couldn't believe she had just offered to spend some time with Moe but found it the only courteous thing to do, given the situation.

"Yeah, sure. That'll be great fun," Moe said sarcastically. His expression softened, though, when he leant in to kiss his grandmother's forehead. Ignoring Dr Ahmed's frown, Moe then sauntered out of the room.

Allura sighed.

Exchanging goodbyes with Fatima, she turned to leave but was interrupted: "Allura, are you going to be long?"

"No, Dr Ahmed. I'll just show Moe a few wards, the garden and probably my office. Can I help you with anything?"

"Just don't waste too much time, please." His tone was harsh. Allura wasn't quite sure what to make of it. Ahmed never interfered with what Allura did, nor did he ever order her around that way. In fact, lately he had been unusually sweet with her. On most days, it felt like he was giving her preferential treatment over the centre's long-term staff.

"Yes, Dr Ahmed. I won't be long."

As they walked out, Moe looked at Allura and smirked. "So what's up with Mister Doctor here?"

"What do you mean?"

"He seems constipated. What's up with his bossy attitude?"

"He's actually a very sweet guy. You just don't know him. He's just a bit too serious at times, that's all."

"Ummm, I guess you would know better."

Allura decided to change topics. "So hey, Moe, what's up with your new look? I like it."

Moe blushed. "Yeah, uh, I did it for my grandma. I could keep this style though, if you think it looks better."

Allura laughed. "Well, it does make you look chic. But it's your decision."

"So what have you been up to other than working in this old people's home?"

"It's a healthcare centre for the elderly!"

"Yeah, whatever. It's a depressing place to work in, if you ask me. So, other than spending time with old people, what do you do for fun?"

"This is my fun! Working with people, meeting new people and learning."

"Learn what exactly? With all due respect, these guys are expired. I mean, they are not much fun to hang out with. You need to mingle with people your own age. Damn, girl, looks like you've got no social life at all."

"I wouldn't say that."

"No? Well, answer this. When was the last time you went out?"

Allura tilted her head as she tried to remember.

"The day I saw you, I went out with my girlfriends to watch a movie!"

"Geez, woman! That was ages ago. You can't be serious. You poor dame. Well, hey, now you got me feeling sorry for you. There's a real cool party Thursday night for some very important people, if you get my drift. Wanna go?"

Allura hesitated. She hadn't been to a party since her parents passed away, but she loved dancing and missed music. The idea sounded like a lot of fun.

"Where is it? And what do you mean, for very important people?"

"It's at a club near school – and before you ask, Jessy and the gang will not be there, I promise. I'm going out with another friend of mine and his girlfriend, who aren't even in our school. Oh, before you ask, they're not like Jessy at all. You'd like them. What I mean by very important people is that not just anyone can go into that place; the guys on the door or the manager have to personally know you, or know of you. So, why don't you join? Adel, my friend, has a car. I can ask him to pass by you, and we can drop you back home safely if you want."

"What time are you going?"

"Well, we don't usually go before ten."

"Ten? That's my curfew; I wouldn't be allowed to go out that late."

"Come on, things don't start heating up before that time. How about I speak to your parents if that makes you feel any better?"

"I live with my aunt."

"Fine, whatever. I'll speak with your aunt."

"Let me think about it."

Moe was delighted; it was a huge improvement from when they'd last spoken. It seemed like Allura had finally decided to give him a chance.

The first thing Allura did when she arrived home was talk to her aunt about the party. Nahed was initially uncomfortable about the timing, but Allura explained that she'd be going to a place that didn't start picking up before ten thirty. She even called Moe, who spoke to Nahed and reassured her that he'd take care of Allura and bring her back home safe.

Nahed was a bit apprehensive but gave her consent, as she wanted to see Allura happy. After sharing full details about the club, its location and even the phone number, Allura promised that she'd make sure her own phone was in easy reach so they could contact each other throughout the night if need be.

Thursday quickly came, and Allura called Moe to go over the details as she got ready.

"Hey, Moe, I'm so excited! We'd better have a good time. Please make sure your friends are cool; I don't want any sort of drama tonight. You mentioned that they have a car, right? Are you sure they can pick me up and drop me off?"

"Yes, Adel's going to pick his girlfriend up first, and then we'll swing by you. Be ready by ten thirty."

"I thought you said we'd be at the club at ten? Moe, I explained to you before, that's far too late for my aunt. She won't allow me to leave the house that late. I have to be back home around midnight!"

"Sheesh, that's way too early. That's basically when people start getting ready in their homes…you know what? It's better than nothing. I'll work it out. I just have to speak to Adel and his girlfriend. They'll probably laugh at me, but I guess that's the price I have to pay to go out with Cinderella here!"

Allura laughed. "You said it. I'm a princess. I'm worth it."

"That you are, my lady!" They both paused for a minute. It was obvious Moe had a thing for Allura, but she chose to ignore it. Moe was not Allura's type. Besides, she couldn't stop thinking of Ahmed. In her eyes, he was a real man, with a proper job and responsibilities. He was in control of things and took his position seriously. He was also passionate about helping others, which was what Allura admired the most about him. Moe was just a spoilt teenager who had nothing on his mind, which was exactly why she agreed to go out with him that night. She wanted to have fun and unwind – something she hadn't done in a very long time.

Earlier that day, Allura had wrapped things up at work. She looked forward to leaving early to get her hair and nails done before the party and had already informed Nurse Josephine about her plans.

She made sure to pass by all the patients she knew to bid them farewell. Sherif was the last patient she visited because she knew saying goodbye to him would take more time.

As she walked into his room, Sherif was sitting on a chair located in front of a window that overlooked the garden. He was sipping his tea and reading a book. A nurse stood close by, getting ready to give him his pills.

"Sherif, hi, it's Allura. Sorry to disturb you. I just wanted to say goodbye. It's my last day at the centre."

"Oh, goodbye, my dear." Sherif was distracted. His condition was getting worse by the day, which saddened Allura greatly. At the same time, she was grateful to be leaving the centre, as she was tired of seeing patients waste away before her eyes.

"Sherif, do you need anything? I'm leaving the centre today, it's my last day."

"No, my dear. Very kind of you to ask."

"OK, Sherif." Allura knelt down beside his chair and held his right hand. "I need something from you, if that's all right?"

"Something from me?"

"Yes, Sherif," she said, smiling.

"What do you need from an old man like me?"

"I need you to take good care of yourself. You are a very special person to my heart. I spoke to you about many things in my life, and there are days when you helped me get through quite a lot of doubts I had. If it doesn't bother you, I'd like to visit you from time to time."

Sherif patted her hand.

"You are more than welcome to come visit me here, my child. That would make me very happy."

"Great! I'll take your word on it and do just that. Now promise me you'll take good care of yourself?"

"I promise."

"And you'll listen to all the nurses here, who all love you very much and want what's best for you?"

"OK."

"I'll miss you, Sherif." Allura's eyes welled with tears as she kissed Sherif's forehead gently. As she was leaving the room she thought about how much she'd really miss her talks with him and hoped that the next time she'd see him he'd be all right. Her parents came to her mind just there. She was not prepared to face yet another tragic loss in her life.

As she walked out, Allura thought about saying goodbye to Ahmed. She wasn't quite sure where to find him but hoped he'd be in the garden. It was where they frequently spoke during her mid-morning breaks.

"You'd better not be leaving without saying goodbye."

Allura jumped slightly. "You startled me! Wow, I should have asked for a million dollars. I was just thinking about you. I'm so happy I ran into you before leaving."

"Is it your last day already? And why so early? It's not even the end of your work day yet."

"I have some things to do today, so I got permission to leave work a little early. Ahmed, I want to thank you for everything you've offered me throughout this whole experience."

"I did nothing. I simply followed your lead," said Ahmed. "I won't say goodbye to you and instead say I hope that I'll see you again soon."

"I'll pass by the centre every now and then, I promise."

"We'll all miss you here, especially some of our patients, like Sherif."

"Oh, he won't even remember me by the time I come back for a visit. I was just up there visiting him, poor man; he's getting worse, by the looks of it."

"Regardless, you bring a smile to his face each time he sees you. Your presence is a joy for some of our patients. Whenever you've got the time, swing by and suggest one of your brilliant picnic ideas. We'll all be more than happy to tag along."

Allura was touched by his words and flattered that he thought about her that way. "Thank you, Dr Ahmed. I will cherish those words forever."

"Dr Ahmed? Didn't we say drop the formalities? Call me Ahmed. Please don't forget, you can reach out to me anytime you need anything, I'll always be here for you, as a friend."

"Thank you, Ahmed. I'll definitely stay in touch, I promise."

As Allura walked out of the centre she had mixed emotions. She was thinking of how much she'd miss Ahmed and wanted to believe that she'd see him again. His words were encouraging and welcoming, and they meant that she was allowed to stay in touch with him. She'd definitely take advantage of that.

The great thing about the centre was that it was in the same neighbourhood as her aunt's house. Even better, there was a beauty parlour along the route where she decided to get her hair and nails done.

Several hours later, she was back home trying on different outfits before finally deciding to wear a tight, off-the-shoulder black dress that ended above her knees. She matched this with dangling earrings and chunky bangles before completing the ensemble with silver peep-toed heels and a matching handbag.

Soon after, Moe phoned to tell her that they were waiting outside. Allura hastily hugged and kissed her aunt good night just as she was exiting the house excitedly.

"Wait a second, missy! I need to see those friends of yours first," voiced Nahed.

"Uh, see them? How? They're in the car waiting for me, Aunt Nahed. I'll be late. Please don't embarrass me. I'm no baby."

"I won't embarrass you; I just need to see them, that's all."

Nahed stepped outside the front porch and waved at the group of friends from a distance. Moe was in the back seat, ready to greet her. Nahed nodded her head and raised her hand. "No, no, no need," she said to Moe. "Stay just where you are. You all have fun tonight. Just take care of my Allura, you hear?"

"Yes, ma'am, we will. Don't worry about her. We'll make it by curfew, I promise," answered Moe as he stuck his head out the car window.

Chapter 11

Don't Judge a Book by Its Cover

Walking towards them, Allura gasped when she caught a close-up sight of the stunning red sports car and well-dressed group.

"Hey guys, how are you?" she said as she crawled into the small back seat.

"Hey beautiful, you look gorgeous! Fancy meeting your aunt tonight too! Now I know where you get your good looks," said Moe with a delightful smile before turning to his friends.

"Oh, hey, this is my friend, Adel, and his girlfriend, Anna. Guys, this is Allura."

"Hi, Allura, nice to meet you," said Adel. He took a peek at Allura through the rear-view mirror as he drove off.

Meanwhile, Anna extended her hand to shake Allura's hand.

"Are we all ready to party or what?" screamed Moe, who was already all hyped up about the night and loved the idea of sitting this close to Allura.

Allura's heart started to race. She hadn't felt this ecstatic in ages and couldn't wait to visit a dance club for the first time in her life, see new faces and dance the night away.

The minute they arrived, Adel parked his ostentatious car in front of the door and handed the car keys to the valet attendant, who seemed to know both Adel and Moe very well. They were obviously frequent customers. The bouncers and club manager who stood by the door also greeted them with warmth and respect as they entered the establishment. They were quickly seated at one of the best tables on the second floor, which offered a perfect view of the dance floor. The club manager invited them to use the club's private room in case they wanted to get more comfortable.

After a few minutes, a waiter showed up at their table to take their orders. Allura was amazed by the service they received all night. She had no idea Moe had such a diverse circle of friends. For all she knew, he was the spoilt little school brat who hung out with a bunch of rude punks who had nothing better to do than to bully people.

Moe and Allura sat down next to one another on the couch. "What would you like to drink?" Moe whispered gently in Allura's ear, giving her goose bumps. Allura had no idea what type of perfume he was wearing, but it just smelt spectacular.

"Orange juice, please," she replied shyly.

Moe laughed and looked towards Adel and Anna. "Hey guys, guess what Allura wants to drink? Orange juice!"

"What's wrong with orange juice?" asked Allura crossly.

"We're at a nightclub, sweetheart. Don't you drink at all?" asked Moe.

"Well, I've tried it a few times, but I'd rather not drink tonight."

"We're here to have fun. Take a few shots. If you can't take it anymore, I'll be the first to stop you, OK? I got your back, I promise!"

"Hmmm, I'm really not that into alcohol. Just as long as I don't get drunk, I guess I can try what you're taking."

"Start off with this. It's called a tequila shot. It's a little sour, but the effect is sweet. It'll get you flying soon enough. Then you can order a bullfrog just like me. That'll chill you out for the rest of the night."

"Like I said, I have no idea what's what, so I'll choose to trust you on this."

Allura quickly downed the shot the way Moe showed her. The burning liquid almost made its way out of her mouth before she forced herself to swallow. She smiled triumphantly when the others cheered at her success.

"This is gross! How on earth do you people drink this crap?"

"Ha-ha, Allura. I think you'll fit in with us beautifully tonight. You're so funny," commented Anna in her East European accent.

Allura laughed. "Seriously, it really is disgusting."

Towards the middle of the night, Allura felt tipsy, yet happy. She felt free and enjoyed the attention she was getting as she writhed her body fluidly to the pulsing beat of the music.

Not long after, the dance floor started to pick up. The music wound its way through her body as the tempo began to speed up. Eyes shut, she began to lose herself to the hypnotic rhythm and unintentionally drifted to the corner of the dance floor, where a man grabbed her waist and started to dirty dance with her. She was so into the music that she decided to let the man touch her. Her hair wildly whipped the air with every move she took.

Moe realised Allura was no longer nearby. He looked for her till he found her dancing with a complete stranger. Gritting his teeth, he headed in their direction, planning how to address the situation without getting into a fight or ending up banned from the club.

"Hey man, it isn't hip taking advantage of a tipsy woman at a dance club. Now if you don't mind, please keep your hands to yourself. That's my girlfriend you're dancing with there," said Moe calmly.

"Sorry, man!" The guy instantly let go of Allura.

Moe realised Allura was on the verge of becoming drunk, so guided her back to the table. "Allura, have some water. You're drunk. Would you like to go to the bathroom and freshen up a bit?"

"I'm not drunk, and I'm not your girlfriend, by the way! I'm having fun. You're just jealous because some other guy had his hands around my waist!"

"Well, maybe I am slightly jealous. But I'm also sticking to my promise and looking out for you."

"I need to sit down. I'm dizzy."

As soon as they sat down on a nearby couch, Allura rested her head on Moe's shoulders. She suddenly felt exhausted from all the dancing and excitement.

"You know what, Moe? You're actually a sweet guy. Not as bad as I thought you were. One should never judge a book by its cover."

"Well, thank you. You're a beautiful person too, Allura, inside and out. You also make me question the type of friends I hang out with, like your bestie, Jessy, for example." Moe sniggered sarcastically. "You know, I stopped hanging out with her completely. You were right about her. She's wacked."

As he was speaking, Allura's head started to slant his way. Moe took this as an opportunity to place his arms around her shoulders and run his fingers down her hair.

"Allura, are you sure you're feeling all right? It's getting late. How about I drop you back home?" Moe was genuinely concerned. He had never seen someone react so strongly after drinking so little alcohol.

"I'm fine. I just need to sit for a bit. I'll be all right. I guess I'm just not used to the alcohol. Thanks, Moe. You're very sweet tonight!"

Allura felt relaxed, excited, happy and attractive. She closed her eyes as she caressed Moe, breathing in his scent. Moe was captivated by how sensual she was and involuntarily moved his face towards hers until their noses almost touched. They were separated by little more than a breath.

Allura smiled shyly as she lifted her eyes to meet his. Moe slowly slid his hands down Allura's lower back and pulled her closer. Her breath hitched when their eyes met. Allura was enjoying the moment and hoped Moe would get straight to the point. She tilted her head to the opposite side, ready for the kiss that Moe didn't hesitate to exchange. He tactfully and gently placed his lips on hers. As they were kissing, Allura gently pulled away. They exchanged another shy smile and hugged each other tight for a few good minutes.

Allura didn't want to make any kind of sense about what was going on. She had no feelings for Moe; it was pure experimentation and lust from her side. She was also drunk, which gave her more courage. She liked kissing Moe, though. He was a good kisser, which made it even more enjoyable.

"Wow, looks like you two lovebirds were in the middle of something! I say get a room!" joked Adel as he approached the two with Anna by his side.

Allura and Moe both smiled bashfully, and the four went back to the dance floor to enjoy the rest of the night. Allura decided to drink water during her last hour at the club in order to sober up. Once she was ready to go home, she still had a slight buzz but felt great.

The next morning, Allura woke up with a severe hangover. She instantly remembered the kiss and slid her body under the covers in shame.

What on earth did I do last night? Oh my God, I kissed Moe, a guy I once disliked and tried to avoid! What on earth was I thinking? Am I that desperate?

She couldn't stop blaming herself for losing control like that but then started to think of the kiss itself. I remember that kiss, though. It was special. He kisses well. But still, I could have kissed anyone else. Why Moe? It must have been the alcohol!

She was still berating herself when Nahed walked into the bedroom, disturbing her thoughts. "So how was your wild night out?" she asked. Usually, she would knock before entering Allura's room, but not this time. Nahed was concerned that Allura might have experimented with a few things the night before and was worried about her decision to let her out in the first place.

Taking a deep breath, Nahed waited for her response. She wanted Allura to have fun but be safe and responsible at the same time.

"It was fun, Auntie Nahed. Thank you for asking, and thank you for allowing me to go. If it's OK, I'd love to go out every now and then with my friends."

"Of course it's OK. Everyone needs to unwind and have fun every now and then. But you need to respect your curfew."

"I'm sorry, I know I was slightly late coming back home last night, it won't happen again, I promise."

Allura's mobile phone suddenly rang. It was Ahmed. Allura breathed a sigh of relief; she was saved by the bell. Her aunt was starting to make her feel uncomfortable with all her inquisitive questions, and Allura didn't like to lie. She would have eventually given in and spilled details about the night.

Nahed had noticed the change in Allura's expression. Pursing her lips, she said: "Attend to your phone call. We'll talk later," before making her way out of the room.

Taking a deep breath, Allura accepted the call.

"Allura, how are you? I've missed seeing you around the centre. Hope all's well?"

"Great, thank you for asking. I am so happy to hear of you – I mean, from you." Allura stuttered, heart pounding and palms sweaty. The last thing she wanted was for Ahmed to hear how anxious and hungover she sounded. Taking a deep breath, she continued: "So, how are things at the centre?"

Ahmed chuckled. "As always, full of ups and downs. The patients miss you already and are all asking about you. Aren't you planning to visit us sometime soon?"

"I'd love to visit you! Just let me know when that's possible." Ahmed definitely made her day. Allura had forgotten about her pounding head and last night's embarrassing kiss.

"You don't need an appointment to visit us. Drop by anytime. How about right now? Are you doing anything?"

"I have to study today, but I promise I'll drop by tomorrow morning."

"That'll be lovely. We can't wait to see you again!"

As she hung up, Allura wondered whether Ahmed had called her because the patients were asking to see her or because he actually missed her being around. She hoped it was the latter and intended to find out during her visit to the centre. She was determined to start getting closer to Ahmed. Kissing Moe seemed to have ignited something within her, and she wanted to explore it and see where it would take her.

Stumbling out of bed, she hastily freshened up before seeking out the family chef and requesting that he bake a sweet potato cake for her to take to the centre the next day. It was the same cake the group had enjoyed on their park outing all those weeks ago, and Allura hoped it would bring a smile to their faces.

Chapter 12

Memories are Impossible to Reproduce

Allura cheerfully greeted everyone as she made her way to the kitchen, cake in hand. *It would be a nice midmorning treat with some tea*, she thought, as she bustled around preparing everything.

Straining to reach the pot at the topmost shelf, she nearly lost her balance when a cheerful voice called out.

"Why, hello there! I heard you were here. How are you?"

Regaining her footing, she turned with an easy smile.

"Hello, Ahmed. It's nice seeing you again."

"If you're not busy, let's grab a coffee or something and sit at the garden, just like old times," said Ahmed, gesturing to the plump cake and myriad of empty cups.

"Um, sure. But I'd like to get back in time to prepare everything for the morning break. Do you think they'd like the cake? Or should I have gotten a chocolate one? I should've, right? I mean, not everyone likes sweet potato cake," Allura rambled nervously.

"Allura! Relax. They'll love it. C'mon. I'd like to catch up before you get mobbed by everyone and forget about me," Ahmed said with a grin.

"I'd never forget about you. I mean, you're dear to me. As a friend! You're a good friend. I'm going to shut up now." Allura's cheeks were on fire.

Ahmed guffawed. "You're a good friend to me too. C'mon, let's go grab that coffee."

Steaming cups in hand, Allura and Ahmed sat in their usual spot within the centre's meditative garden, which evoked the very essence of calmness and peace. It was especially designed to provide a place for retreat and offer a great setting to get away and unwind.

While seated comfortably on a perfectly located bench surrounded by ornamental grass and long-stemmed colourful flowers, Ahmed started opening up about how busy he had been in the past few months and how much he needed a vacation. As he spoke, Allura was struck by just how stressful a doctor's life really was.

After almost an hour of nonstop talk, Ahmed realised that he had spoken for far too long. "Gosh, you must think I'm a crazy person by now! My job is to listen to patients, prescribe medication and offer treatment. Hardly anybody listens to me. You know what, Allura? Despite how young you are, there's something about you that's just so approachable and sincere."

Allura's heart fluttered. It was the first time they had actually had a personal conversation alone. She loved hearing him; the sound of his voice was soothing.

"I thoroughly enjoy listening to you, Ahmed. I am honoured you feel that way about me. Your dedication and selfless approach at work are admirable. I'd probably have gone bananas by now if I were in your shoes."

Ahmed laughed. He felt serene around Allura and was curious to know more about her.

"I've probably made it sound worse than it really is. Anyway, enough about me. You're so kind, allowing me to prattle on like that. So now that you've heard my endless complaints, what's your story?"

"What do you mean?"

"I mean, how is school treating you? How are your friends? You mentioned once something about swimming. Are you on a team? You know, I don't think you've really told me much about your life. You're like this mysterious creature that suddenly arrived at the centre – to our luck, of course," said Ahmed with a shrug.

Allura took a deep breath. Fidgeting slightly under Ahmed's intense gaze, she focused on a distant tree. She wasn't sure where to start. It almost felt like they were getting acquainted for the very first time. She decided to let the words come out as she felt them.

"Well, you know I'm seventeen. I've just started my last year of high school. Before that, though, I actually lived in Abu Dhabi, in the UAE…do you know it?" At Ahmed's nod, she continued: "I moved here after my parents died. They were in a car accident. Don't be sad. I'm better now. I live with my aunt, who treats me as one of her own. I adore her, and she's become my whole world. I think I'm adjusting well, given the circumstances."

Ahmed sighed, trying to look unaffected. "I'm so sorry, Allura. This must be very hard for you."

"It is. It's very hard, especially since it was around this time last year when it happened, but with each passing day, I get stronger by the grace of God. I love them and miss them, and I cherish each and every single memory I have of them. But I'm trying to survive. Not one day passes without them crossing my mind, I'm trying my best to stay true to them and make them proud, but you know, I do make mistakes along the way. I'm trying my best. You learn to accommodate to the situation, I guess." Tears started rolling from Allura's eyes.

"Oh, Allura, trust me. They are proud of you. Who wouldn't be? You're such a strong young lady. To have gone through such a tragic situation and still be a rather upbeat person means you're much stronger than you probably realise."

"You know, Ahmed, when I see families in the park or walking down the street or something, as corny as this sounds, a part of me wants to walk up to them and tell them to cherish every moment they've got together. You never know what'll happen in life," she said, wiping away her tears.

"My parents were amazing people. Even though we'd sometimes fight, they were always there for me. Every night I'd curl up in my mother's arms and listen to her soft voice as she read aloud to me. That was a habit starting when she was pregnant with me that continued till I grew older. I think that's where I developed my love of reading. The bond between us was indescribable. She sacrificed a lot, and her patience…well, I've never met anyone quite like her!

"They both taught me so much. I still sometimes hear their voices. I've run into random rooms thinking they're there, but it turns out to be the sound of the television or something."

Casually, she brushed back the wisps of dark hair that had escaped her ponytail. "Dad was rather overprotective, but I know he was looking out for me. Despite his busy schedule, he'd actually spend quality time with Mum and me. He helped my mother with the smallest things. He was respectful towards her and always taught me how important it is to respect my elders. He particularly spoke highly about women. He'd say, 'It is thanks to a female that life is moving on in beautiful directions. They are the mothers, the wives, the sisters. It is a woman who sacrifices, multitasks and gives meaning to life, and it is she who inspires a man. It's a fact, a female helps drive a man forward.'

"God rest his soul, Daddy really did mean what he said. Not once did I hear him raise his voice at my mother or disrespect her in any way. He was always very decent and calm. I wish I could marry someone half as amazing as he was one day!"

"He sounds like he was a very wise man, respecting you and your mum like that. I'm not sure you'll ever be able to find a man so dedicated these days, to be honest. But I'm sure the best is yet to come for you."

"That he was." Looking down at her wristwatch, Allura realised how fast time had flown.

"And you call yourself a chatter-box? Look at me now, going on and on like that."

Ahmed knew Allura was hurting. She had so many bottled-up emotions inside her that needed to be expressed. He listened contemplatively as the teenager released her pent-up emotions. He found himself admiring Allura's strength and her determination to not let her circumstances destroy her.

"I hope you don't mind me hugging you right now. I've been told I'm a good hugger."

Allura was taken aback. She had dreamed of the day when Ahmed would touch her but became almost painfully shy.

Without waiting for a response, Ahmed reached over, flexed his arms, and enveloped her for a quick embrace. Allura subconsciously tightened her hold on his arms before slowly releasing herself. Both blushed lightly and looked away as they processed the intimate moment.

Clearing his throat, Ahmed said: "I can't even go on to imagine how hard that must have been for you, especially at your young age. How did you snap out of it? I mean, did you snap out of it at all? How are you feeling about all this now?"

As if relieved with Ahmed's encouragement to carry on talking, Allura without hesitation went on. "When I first learnt about the news, I felt lifeless, incomplete and lonely. It felt like I had died with them that day and possibly for a good few days, even months. But now, my views have completely changed. I notice beauty in the smallest things, even silly things like the colour of flowers or the sound of children laughing."

"Amen to that. I'm so happy to hear it."

"After everything I've gone through though, I can't help but ask myself what the world has come to. I mean, why the hatred, the discrimination, the wars, the battles – why anything bad? If only people remembered the limited amount of time they had in this place, they'd appreciate life a bit more and choose to live wisely and peacefully for the rest of their days."

Ahmed pursed his lips approvingly.

Allura exhaled as she continued: "When a friend shows me a bracelet her mother has just brought her or complains about how her dad embarrassed her, I feel angry and jealous. They're taking so much for granted and have so many experiences that I'll never have. It hurts. I want to shake them and tell them that these stupid things will be the things they'll treasure the most when their parents are gone!"

Amazed at her astuteness, Ahmed reached out to hold her hand. She spoke from the heart, and with such eloquence.

"My mother's favourite quote about life always comes to my mind. It goes as follows: 'Time is like a river. You cannot touch the same water twice, because the flow that has passed will never pass again.' It's that simple, people should be more grateful and loving towards one another, especially towards those closest to them, their family members most importantly."

"That's beautiful – and so true."

"On a more positive note, I'm now blessed to have an amazingly supportive aunt and good friends. I just, you know, keep myself busy as best I can."

Still holding onto her hand, Ahmed sympathised.

"God knows, I've gotten into my fair share of arguments with my own parents. Maybe I should start spending more time with them," he said in a humorous tone, trying to get Allura's mind off things as he rolled his eyes in sarcasm.

The sound of far-off laughter broke the heavy atmosphere.

"Thanks, Ahmed, for listening to me. You really are a good shrink," said Allura with a wet giggle.

Ahmed grinned. "Well, I'm not here as your shrink. I'm here as your friend. You listened to what I had to say too, you know!"

"Yeah, but you were speaking about work. I was talking about heavy, morbid stuff."

"It's the same thing, Allura. We both opened up to each other about our feelings, and I hope that you know that you can come to me and talk about anything, anytime. If I can, I'll try to help. If not, I'll just be a shoulder for you to cry on, so to speak."

"I'd love that. But if we're going to start having sessions like this, then it's only fair I offer advice too. Starting with, get a life! There's so much more to do than worry about the centre. Go for a coffee with friends, go clubbing, go skydiving…just go and do something different. You're far too young to engross yourself like this."

Ahmed laughed. "You think I'm this sad, lonely doctor stuck in this centre, huh? Wasting my youth away?"

"Well, you're not getting any younger. It might do you some good to see other people your own age," Allura teased.

"Is that right? Well, what's your prescription, then?"

"Do you know that sports club nearby the centre, the one around the corner from the shawarma shop? I've started going there to work on my swimming. How about you meet me there and we can do something together, or whatever?"

"Sounds like a plan!"

Smoothing her hair, Allura glanced down at her wrist again.

"Oh wow. It's so late! Is there still time to give everyone some cake?"

"Hm? Oh, yeah, I think there's about twenty minutes left. I'll help. After you, m'lady," Ahmed said with a mock bow.

Allura giggled. "Thank you, kind sir."

As she walked slowly in front of him, Ahmed leered slightly at the stunning beauty before him. He captured the moment in his mind and wasn't about to forget it. She was even more beautiful than he had remembered. Or had his feelings become more intense since Allura confessed her tragic life story?

Unbeknownst to him, Allura was grappling with her own conflicting feelings. In her eyes, Ahmed was a handsome man with a pleasing personality. It seemed that he might also like her, which was something she had yearned for all those weeks ago. Yet, she had kissed Moe the other night and also felt something for him. What did all that mean? She was confused and intensely guilt-ridden. She kept thinking to herself: *This wasn't the behaviour of good girls, nor was it the way her parents raised her.*

Putting the swirling thoughts out of her mind, Allura focused on enjoying the rest of the day with her elderly friends and the nurses who cared for them.

Returning home, Allura decided to take Bassel's advice about how she felt. Opening her laptop, she typed out a quick e-mail:

***

Hey, Bassel,

I hope you're doing well back there! I miss you around. Miss our long talks and our fun swimming sessions. I'm sure you're very busy getting ready for that competition you told me about, but I need some advice. I've met someone, and I think I'm kind of dating another boy. I'm very confused about both. I feel guilty because I have feelings for one and am physically attracted to the other. Does that make me a really bad person? Both guys make me feel great in their own different ways. What do I do, Bassel? Please guide me as you always do. Let me know how you're doing. I want to know all your news!

Love, A

***

A few hours later, Bassel responded.

***

Hey there! You've changed since I've last seen you. You're becoming a wild cookie. Wish I was there! Too bad you weren't that wild around me. LOL! Kidding.

I'd be lying if I didn't say I was jealous right now. But for what it's worth, here's my advice: listen to both your heart and mind. What does your heart tell you? Which one of them do you want to spend the most time with? Which one of them gets you the most, like the fact that you're probably stressing about your final year of high school and that you don't have much time on your hands?

There's also that scholarship you talked about. To get it, you've got to get good grades, and it'll definitely be hard to focus if you're worrying about two boys. Anyway, I know you can be rather stubborn about things. In the end, you'll always make the right choice.

As for me, well, I'm still practising really hard. I'm seeing someone now; we've been together for almost three weeks.

She's my first real girlfriend, so I'm very excited about it. I guess that's all my news. Till I hear back from you, take good care of yourself!

Regards, Bassel

***

After reading his e-mail, Allura became even more confused. What did Bassel mean? Should she forget about Ahmed and Moe and focus on her studies, or should she pursue these exciting new emotions? A part of her was slightly jealous as well. She and Bassel had almost started dating last year, and now it seemed like he had moved on and almost forgotten all about her.

Punching her pillow in annoyance, she decided to stop thinking so hard. She was a good girl, like Bassel said, and was confident that when the time came, she'd make the right decision. In the meantime, she'd just go with the flow and deal with whatever life threw her way.

Chapter 13

The Library

It had been two weeks since Allura had met Moe at the club, spilled her innermost thoughts to Ahmed, and reached out to Bassel for advice about the confusing situation.

Studying at the library, Allura ignored what seemed to be the thousandth phone call from Moe. She had no idea what to say to him or even how to act around him anymore. Hopefully, he'd get the hint and leave her alone.

Before she knew it, Moe had showed up at the library looking for her.

"Hey, Allura, can we talk?" He was adamant for some sort of closure.

"Shush!" whispered Allura, who at the time was absorbed in a chapter in her biology book in preparation for an upcoming exam. "Talking isn't allowed in the library. Let's step outside; give me a minute."

Moe moaned a disappointed groan. "What? Is that all you can come up with after ignoring me for so long? Are you avoiding me on purpose or something?"

At that point, heads started to turn their way.

"I said, meet me outside. I don't want to get into trouble with the librarian."

"Yea, right. I'll wait for you outside, and you'll never show up. Then I'll look like an idiot. I'll stay right here until you tell me why you've been ignoring my calls."

His raised voice began irritating other pupils, who started to whisper about the situation.

"Shut up, Moe. People are looking. Fine, let's go," Allura hissed angrily.

As soon as they stepped outside, Moe cornered her.

"So?"

"Look, Moe, I don't want to lead you on. I want to stay friends with you. I'm not interested in anything else, and that kiss was just plain wrong! It was the alcohol acting out and not how I really feel about you. Hope that answers your question?"

"Look, I know you don't have feelings for me, and I'm fine with that. I have no issues staying just friends with you, but don't avoid me like that. It's just not nice!"

"I'm sorry, Moe. You're right, but I was just…I was just embarrassed from the other night."

"It's all right, Allura. I'm a big boy. I can handle rejection! I just don't want to lose what we have – call it whatever you want, friendship, special friendship, mates, buddies, whatever," he said with a bitter smile.

Allura looked at him sadly.

"Moe, I haven't known you for too long, and to be honest, I didn't want to lead you on or something. I'm really focusing on my studies right now."

"That's fine. Just don't forget to have fun every now and then. Speaking of which, there's a house party on Friday at Adel's place. You remember Adel, the guy who was out with us at the club?"

"Yea, Adel and Anna. I wasn't that drunk!"

"No need to get prissy. I don't care if you were sober, tipsy or blackout drunk. Anyway, he's got this huge beach house and, like, a small private stretch of beach. He's throwing a party for close friends next Friday and told me to invite you. It's nearly two hours away from Cairo, in an area called El Ain Al Sokhna. Do you think your aunt will let you go?"

"I'm not sure. It's pretty far away."

"Then don't tell her! Just say you're going to one of the hotels to sit by the pool all day with your friends from school. We'll leave there by six, so you'll be home way before curfew."

Allura fidgeted uncomfortably. She had never lied to her aunt before and was actually looking forward to spending some quality time with Ahmed over the weekend.

"C'mon, live a little! You can't spend your life hiding away behind books. People will think you're a hermit or something!"

"I don't know. Let me think about it. I'll let you know tonight or tomorrow."

"OK, but remember the blast we had in the club? Multiply that by like a thousand! That's how awesome this beach party's going to be. Unwind a bit, woman!"

With that, Moe sauntered off, leaving Allura to her thoughts. It was true, she did have a blast with Moe and his friends the other night, and was tempted to go to the party. But then she thought about her aunt. Allura didn't want to push her luck and doubted that Nahed would agree to an all-day beach party located almost two hours away from Cairo anyway, especially with the exams approaching. The last thing she wanted to do was to scandalise her aunt.

Allura headed home straight after school. Despite not being hopeful, she decided to give it a try and speak to her aunt. Just as she was about to launch into her prepared speech, Allura was startled to see that Nahed had company. She was seated with her friend Gladdis at the patio, enjoying a cup of tea and some cake.

"Hello, Allura. Do you need something, dear? Why don't you come and say hello to your Aunt Gladdis?" said Nahed upon noticing her loitering in the doorway.

"Hello, Aunt Nahed, Aunt Gladdis. How are you both doing?"

"Fine, Allura. You look so much better since I last saw you. How are things with you?" asked Gladdis with a warm smile.

"I'm doing well, thank you, Aunt Gladdis. Auntie, can I please speak to you in private?"

"Gladdis is not a stranger, Allura. You may speak in front of her. What is it, dearest?"

Allura started to question whether she should make up a story about Friday or tell the truth. She decided to tell the truth, hoping that Aunt Gladdis' presence would embarrass Nahed a bit and possibly get her to agree.

"Well, my friends are going to El Ain Al Sokhna this Friday to spend the whole day at the beach. It's about two hours away from Cairo. I was wondering whether, well, if I could join them."

"Hmmm, I see. And who exactly are your friends, Allura?"

"Do you remember the group I went out with last week? That same group. Moe, Anna and Adel."

"Till what time are we talking about?"

"I won't be late. I'll try my best to be here by eight o'clock. Is that all right?"

"Who's driving exactly? You know that road could be dangerous!"

"Adel, Aunt Nahed. He's older and very mature. Above all, he drives really well. Besides, that's his beach house we are going to, and he's hosting a lot of people, so I doubt he'll want to jeopardise his own life!" Allura giggled.

Nahed and Gladdis didn't seem entertained by the joke.

"Fine! Just make sure you answer my phone calls. And call me the second you arrive and the minute you leave from there, OK?"

Allura couldn't believe her luck. She thought to herself, *That was easy!*

It was obvious that Nahed wanted to do all it took to make Allura happy and had good intentions. She also trusted Allura and didn't imagine she was up to anything bad.

"Thank you! You're the best auntie ever! I promise to stay in touch with you by phone the second I arrive and before I leave."

Allura kissed her aunt loudly on the cheek. "I'm so excited. This is amazing. I love you, Aunt Nahed. I'm so lucky to have you!"

When Allura was out of sight, Gladdis turned to face her old friend. "Are you insane, Nahed? You're letting a seventeen-year-old go that far away? What if something happened to her? Do you even know who these friends are?"

"I saw them once when they took Allura for a night out a few weeks ago. Anyway, I trust her, and it'll be good for her to get out and have some fun."

"That's very wrong, Nahed. She's such a sweet girl, and so naive! She could be taken advantage of! You need to push for more information about their exact plans and ask to meet those friends of hers before letting them whisk her away. Perhaps call their parents. Are there going to be any grownups around?"

"I didn't think about all that. Still, my Allura is a good girl. She's dedicated to graduating from school with high grades, entering university and starting a career of her own. In any case, every successful person experimented with something at some point of their lives. Why should Allura be any different? Plus, this shows that I trust her, so she won't try to sneak out or do anything illegal."

"This is not about Allura! This is about other people around her. How do you know who they are? You know what, Nahed? Stay in denial! But I tell you, you should be more inquisitive next time! Do you know what mothers do with their teenage daughters? They actually spy on them to make sure they're kept safe! It's only natural, Nahed!"

"Perhaps you're right. She's been through so much though, and she's been a model student and teenager. Why shouldn't she be allowed to experience some sort of excitement in her life?" Nahed replied defensively.

"It's your decision, my dear. Just keep your eyes and ears open."

"I know, Gladdis. I know." Nahed sighed before returning to her tea.

Chapter 14

The Beach Party

Allura squealed in excitement as she shut her bedroom door. Not wanting to tempt fate, she quickly dialled Moe's number.

"Guess what? My aunt agreed for Friday! Isn't that cool? So what do I bring, and who's picking me up? Make sure there's a girl in the car, because my aunt won't like me driving in a car with just guys."

"That's great news! I'll be passing by you with Adel and Anna again. Just bring your swimsuit and spare clothes. We'll be spending most of our time either in Adel's villa or by the sea."

"Cool! Will do just that. Can't wait!"

For the rest of the week, Allura was on her best behaviour, both as a thank-you to her aunt and to prove that she wasn't slacking off. In addition to homework and projects, Allura also helped out with random chores around the house.

That morning, Allura woke up at six-thirty, anxious to get ready for her big day out to the beach. She was excited about meeting new people, dancing, and showing off her summer attire, which she definitely had the figure for. She chose to wear a white, netted bikini set that flattered her caramel skin alongside a tropical-inspired sarong tied around the waist barely covering her hips, a gauzy shirt and flip-flops. She complemented her simple yet stylish outfit with humble, waterproof makeup. She knew it would be an all-day event and wanted to look the part.

Finally, it was time for Moe and his friends to pick her up. As Allura walked out the door, Nahed tried to insist on giving her additional spending money. Allura refused with a smile and hug.

"Morning, guys. Thanks for picking me up again," she greeted the group with a bubbly smile.

"No worries. Let's hit the road!" said Adel as he pumped up the music.

Allura giggled as she swayed to the beat of the hypnotic melodies. Before long, they had passed several police checkpoints and were on their way.

"OK, who wants a beer? Adel? Anna? Allura?" Moe asked as he opened the large duffel bag stashed under his legs.

"Isn't it illegal to drink and drive? Adel shouldn't drink that beer!" Allura said, shocked.

"Nah, we're good. We passed all the major police checkpoints. There aren't any more. The desert road is clear from here. Drink and enjoy. We need to get our buzz on before the party," suggested Moe.

Allura bit her lip in hesitation. She didn't want to look like a party pooper, yet she worried about getting into trouble. Glancing up, she saw Moe waving the bottle with a teasing smirk on his face. Rolling her eyes, she accepted it and laughed when they cheered.

Anna and Moe started to move excitedly when Adel pumped the music even louder, which was inspirational and perfect for a road trip. Everyone in the car, including Allura, started to get into the party mode.

"Dude, you know what would be perfect now?" asked Adel, glancing at Moe, who was in the passenger seat.

"I know what you're thinking, man. But Allura ain't used to this stuff, and we don't want to scare her," answered Moe hesitantly.

Anna laughed. "Come on! You talk as if Allura is some baby. She's a grown-up woman, for crying out loud. How come you don't think of me that way? What's your problem? Get on with it and spark up that joint!"

Allura had no idea what they were talking about and was curious about the strangely shaped cigarette in Moe's hand. Soon it was being passed around, filling the car with a strange-smelling smoke.

"What's that? It doesn't smell like a normal cigarette. I feel dizzy from the smell of this crap!" complained Allura.

Anna laughed, waving the joint in front of the younger woman's face.

"This, my dear baby girl, is a happy cigarette. It gets you relaxed and blissful."

"Oh my God, are you guys crazy? You want to go to jail? Please, put that thing out. I am not into this stuff at all and don't want to be a part of it. Please throw it out before I jump out of this car right now."

Allura started to panic. She wasn't sure what she had gotten herself into.

"Relax, will you? It's just a rolled-up cigarette. If you don't want to take a puff, that's your choice. Don't ruin our day just because you're acting like you're some saint or something," said Anna.

Allura quietened down. The smoke's effects were already coursing through her body, resulting in a low buzz. She was relieved when they finally arrived and resolved to not let her friends' actions ruin the rest of her day.

Taking in the large waterfront villa and glittering sea beyond, Allura couldn't contain her excitement. Eyes darting around, she became captivated by the expansive scenery. Alongside lounge chairs, colourful beanbags and a stack of beach supplies, there were numerous barbecue stations and bars dotted around the pool and on the shore.

Ignoring her companions and other partygoers, Allura headed into the water for a refreshing dip. Her eye firmly on the horizon, she didn't realise just how far she had gone.

Moe watched her as she swam further and further out to sea. He was worried she wouldn't be able to make it back again and asked Adel whether he could borrow one of his jet skis. At that point, Allura was floating in the water with her head just above the surface of the sea. Her eyes were shut and her ears halfway immersed beneath the water. It was peaceful down there, and she was able to relax and forget about her uncomfortable situation.

Letting her mind wander, Allura hadn't noticed that Moe had been trying to get her attention.

"Allura! Allura!" shouted out Moe as he approached her, but she still didn't hear his calls.

Moe then decided to drive around where she floated and splash her with some water to catch her attention. The waves and roar of the nearby jet ski disturbed her peace of mind.

"Moe! What the—? Can't you see I want to be alone?"

"You've been out here for ages. Sue me, I was worried. C'mon, let's head back. Get a couple of refreshing drinks and some delicious food and relax by the pool."

"How far do I need to swim to make myself understood?"

Allura was irritated. She liked Moe but didn't quite feel comfortable about being at the party anymore.

"Come back with me. We'll talk. I don't get why you're alone. We're here to have fun and chill out. Why are you being a party pooper?"

"Moe, please! I just need to be alone for a while!"

"You don't come to a beach party and then decide you'd like to be left alone. What's your problem?" Moe asked, irritated.

"I'm dizzy, thanks to your happy cigarette! I'm not exactly in the mood to talk!"

"That doesn't make you dizzy. It gets you high. You're dizzy because you've been floating in the water with your ears half covered in this heat for a good ten minutes."

"Whatever. Leave me alone. Just go!" Allura yelled as she tried to swim away but was blocked by the jet ski.

"Look, just climb aboard, and we'll talk. We don't have to go back, OK?" Moe said.

Allura huffed.

"I bet you don't know how to get on one from the water," he taunted.

"Of course I do! I used to jet ski in Abu Dhabi all the time!"

"Prove it," Moe challenged.

"Fine!" Allura pulled herself up easily and straddled the jet ski. "Happy?" she asked, winding her arms around his waist.

"Very, my fit little lady. Now hold on tight!"

Soon, the sounds of their shrieking laughter filled the air as Moe attempted to show off some tricks. By the time they headed back to shore, the teenagers had attracted an audience.

"Yo, Adel, who's that chick hanging out with Moe?" asked Loay, one of Adel's more notorious friends, as he gestured with his drink.

Adel laughed. "She's cute, huh? Dude, she's out of your league. Forget it. Besides, she's with Moe, man."

"Moe?" Loay laughed. "That's a first! There is no way a fine young dame like that is with Moe. Are you kidding me? Who is she, anyway?"

"I think they go to the same school. And from where I'm standing, it sure looks like they're dating," Adel said with a shrug. "This is the second time we've hung out. The first time was when we went to Mesmerise. She's the one I told you about, who can't hold her liquor but can burn up the dance floor. Y'know, she complained about our smoking on the way over here. Talk about innocent, huh?"

"Thanks, bro. That's useful information. Now watch me put the moves on her. She'll be mine by the end of the night, I guarantee it."

"Man, you're full of it!" said Adel, laughing. "Whatever, have fun!" he said as he walked off to search for his girlfriend.

Loay frowned as he approached the laughing couple relaxing at the front patio. Spying a nearby bar, the twenty-five-year-old smirked.

"Here you go, guys!" said Loay as he handed them bottles of beer.

"Hey man, thanks. You're Loay, right?" asked Moe half-heartedly.

"Yeah, man. You're Moe, right? I've seen you a few times at parties with Adel." Loay shook his hand before turning to Allura.

"Hi there, gorgeous, and what's your name?" he asked, grinning.

"Hi, I'm Allura."

"Cool, can I join you guys? What you up to?"

"Nothing much, man. We're just chilling," replied Moe sternly.

"I'm gonna lie down on the sand. You're welcome to join me," said Allura as she sipped her beer.

Loay's eyes grew wide behind his sunglasses. Didn't she know just how sexy she looked, stretched out like that? He glanced at Moe and noticed the teen staring unabashedly at the beauty before him. Loay glared. Allura was his, damn it! And he wasn't going to let some teenage punk get in the way of seducing her.

"So, Allura, I haven't seen you at a party before. Doesn't seem like this is your kind of thing. Are you having fun today?" he asked with feigned innocence.

"Yeah, you're right, this isn't really my thing. But I had fun on the jet ski. Thanks, Moe," she replied, as she turned to look at Moe, who she was starting to warm up to again.

Smiling back at Allura, Moe sat back and took a hard look at the older man. He looked like a movie star, but there was something dark lurking beneath the surface. Whatever it was, Moe's protective instincts had kicked into high gear. He knew he needed to get Allura away from Loay.

"Hey, Allura, let's dance. C'mon, you love this song!"

Without hesitation, Allura stood up. "Yea, you're right, I love that song! Let's go!"

The day's excitement had adrenaline coursing through Allura's veins, giving her an extra boost of energy, which was amplified by the DJ's music selection.

As Moe and Allura headed to dance, Loay steered them towards a bar. "Let's get some drinks before you go dancing! What'll you have?"

"Oh, a margarita for me, please!" said Allura, body moving to the upbeat tempo.

"What about you, Moe?" Loay asked.

"Nothing, man. I'm good!" answered Moe abruptly.

"Nah, that can't be right. I'll get you a strong daiquiri cocktail. Looks like you need one!"

Turning away, Loay sprinkled some sedatives into their drinks. He was going to get Allura alone, one way or another.

"Allura, I'm not comfortable with that guy. He's way older than we are, he seems to be a complete moron, and he's majorly into you. Something doesn't feel right about him," said Moe, as he stood opposite to Allura, leaning against the bar's wooden edge.

"You're just paranoid. He seems fun! Didn't you tell me to enjoy the party? Now who's being a downer?" Allura teased.

"Allura, this is serious. He's hitting on you, and I don't like it!"

"Oh, ha-ha, so you're jealous! Awww, that's so adorable, Moe. My big, strong protector." Allura giggled as she tipsily patted his cheek.

Moe swatted her hand away in irritation. But before he could take her away, Loay had arrived with the drinks.

"Here you go. Bottoms up!"

Allura took a sip of her margarita before putting it down at a nearby table while Moe chugged his daiquiri in frustration and threw the empty glass onto the sand. Grabbing her hand, Moe dragged Allura to the centre of the dance floor, missing Loay's evil smirk.

Several songs later, Moe started to feel drowsy and restless.

"Hey, Allura, let's take a break. How about we rest a bit on the couch here?"

"No! I love this song! You go rest, I'm good!"

By then, Loay had smoothly made his way through the crowd, ready to strike.

"Allura! There you are!" Loay said as he slickly came between the two friends. "You forgot your drink on the table," he added, handing it over.

"Oh, thanks! I totally forgot about it," she said before taking a big gulp. Glancing up, Allura jumped in surprise. It seemed like Loay's eyes had glittered menacingly for a second before the light changed and they returned to their normal brown colour.

Turning around, she looked for Moe but couldn't see past the crushing throng of people to where her friend was already passed out on one of the loungers.

Whipping back to Loay, she staggered.

"Uh, I suddenly don't feel very good," she groaned.

"What's wrong? Do you feel sick? You hardly drank anything," Loay commented, surprised that the sedative had kicked in that fast.

"I don't know. I'm a good girl. I don't drink. I don't smoke. I'm a good girl! Please don't tell my aunt I drank and smoked!" she wailed in confusion, much to his amusement.

"OK, yes, yes, you are a good girl. Let's get you freshened up, and you can lie down for a bit, OK?"

"Uh, OK, I guess, I dunno…"

Allura rested her head on Loay's shoulders as he carried her to the bathroom, where she scrambled to reach the toilet bowl. Sitting next to her, Loay soothed the hysterical teen as he held her hair back. As Allura sat back, she promptly blacked out.

When she came to, Allura screamed. She was completely naked in a strange room and had no recollection of how she had gotten there.

Chapter 15

The Confrontation

Panting for relief, Allura had finally lurched her way to the hotel doorway. Catching her breath, she hastily searched for the phone in her back pocket.

"Hello? Ahmed? Ahmed! Are you still there?"

"Yes, Allura. Don't worry, I'm here. Where are you right now?"

Relieved to hear her friend's voice again, Allura took another long, deep breath.

"I've just arrived at the hotel entrance. What do I do now?"

"Perfect. Things are going your way so far. OK, now you have two choices. Either head towards the reception, book a room and try to lie down and relax, then call me – which I'd honestly prefer you pick as an option – or head to the nearest café, drink something, and wait there till I arrive. Remember, try to avoid taking a shower or bathing until the doctor sees you, he will need to collect evidence that you were raped."

"Ahmed, I left my bag with all my belongings at the party, and I can't think or communicate with anyone right now. My head is heavy; I think I'm still drunk or stoned. I just feel very dizzy and strange!"

"How much did you drink, Allura? What did you drink exactly?"

"From what I recall…I think a beer and two margaritas."

"That's not enough to get you that drunk! Anyway, we'll talk when I see you. Approach the receptionist and put him on the phone. I'll talk to him!"

Allura did just that. Not noticing the glares directed at her unkempt appearance, she limped towards the reception and handed over her phone without uttering a single word.

"Hello, Rami speaking," answered the confused receptionist as he put the phone to his ear.

"Good afternoon Rami. My name is Dr Ahmed Barakat, owner of the Barakat Centre for the Elderly, located in Cairo. Are you familiar with my father, Dr Shawki Barakat?" Ahmed's father was a renowned public figure in Egypt, almost everyone had heard of or knew of him.

"Yes, of course, sir. I know Dr Barakat, a reputable figure. How may I help you, sir?" asked the courteous receptionist.

"That's my cousin right there in front of you. She's feeling very sick, and I was supposed to pick her up a few hours ago and ran late. Could you be kind enough to accommodate her in one of your hotel suites till I get there? If you have an e-mail address, I'll forward you my credit card details and personal credentials right away as a guarantee."

Ahmed had no idea who he was talking to and didn't want to risk the receptionist rejecting his request, which was exactly why he preferred not getting into details about Allura's assault.

"But sir, we require her passport or identification in order to book a room for her. I'm afraid I can't help you."

"Do this as a personal favour for me, and I promise to compensate you. If you'd like, I can call the hotel management. My cousin has just come through an unfortunate incident, and I really need your help with this!"

"But sir, as mentioned earlier, I need a copy of her identification. Not to mention the fact that she looks extremely young, and she's unaccompanied by an adult…"

Ahmed remembered that copies of Allura's passport and identification documents were with his Human Resources department, since she had worked at the centre earlier.

"Fair enough. I'll make a phone call and send you a copy of her passport alongside the room payment and my passport details as a guarantee. Just keep her out of sight till I call you back. Please give me your personal contact details. I need five minutes, and I'll call you back – or actually, just keep this phone nearby. Rami, listen. I know you're doing your job, but let me ask you this. Do you have a sister?"

"Yes sir, I have three sisters."

"Consider her one of your sisters, and take good care of her. She's young, and as I mentioned earlier, she's vulnerable right now. Please do this for me. I promise and repeat, I will compensate you really well when I see you! If need be, put your manager on the line, and I'll explain the situation to him."

"That's fine, sir. No need for that. We will accommodate her; just send me her passport or identification details at your earliest possible convenience, please."

Ahmed was convincing, and the receptionist had already noticed that something was out of the ordinary. Allura looked abused. Her eyeliner was all smudged, she had bruises all over her arms and face, and her hair was a mess. She also looked like she was in a daze.

Handing over the phone back to the distraught teenager, the receptionist offered Allura some water.

"Miss, please feel free to wait in our nearby restaurant till Dr Ahmed sends me your passport and identification credentials. If there's anything you need, please let me know. I'm working till nine tonight."

Allura felt slightly reassured with the receptionist's hospitality.

"Thank you. What did he tell you?" asked Allura in a shaky tone. Her eyes were puffed up from crying, and her speech was still slurred from the sedative.

The receptionist could tell she was under the influence.

"He will call me back, miss. Just hand me the phone once he does," he replied calmly.

"Thank you!"

Allura dragged herself to the nearby café, where only a few guests were seated. The setting put her mind at ease for the time being.

Half an hour later, Ahmed called Allura.

"Allura, darling, I am very close. I'm less than an hour away, and luckily traffic is smooth. Put the receptionist on the line again, please."

Allura handed the phone to the receptionist and waited as he spoke to Ahmed.

"Miss, Dr Ahmed would like to speak with you. I will book a room for you immediately; it will only take a few minutes."

Allura grabbed the phone. "Ahmed, what's going on? Please come quickly."

"I'll be there before you know it. The second the receptionist hands you the key, go inside the room and try to calm yourself down. Put on some soft music or watch a movie. Do anything to try to get your mind off things for the time being. I promise you everything will be fine!"

"How can everything be fine? I was raped, and I have no idea how or when it happened. It's as if I was drugged!"

"Allura, please try to calm down. Just go up to your room, and we'll talk in detail when I see you. I promise I won't let this go till we get to the bottom of it. Just try to relax for now and stay out of sight. Please don't waste time. Did any of those drunken imbeciles happen to see you come into the hotel?"

"I have no idea. I was barely able to drag myself to reach this hotel. I have no idea how I managed to get here. My legs are numb, and my body doesn't feel right. I'm scared, Ahmed. Please come fast," cried Allura.

"I will. I promise, I am on the way. Just do as I say: grab those keys and go up to the room till I get there!"

Rami quickly booked Allura into the first available room. Despite her unbalanced steps, Allura declined the receptionist's offer to escort her personally to the room. She didn't trust anyone at that point.

She could feel tremors in her body. Her hands shaking, she hurriedly unlocked the door and reached for the light switch. She then involuntarily slid down the floor, leaning against the door that she made sure to lock several times behind her.

Huddled up in the corner of the doorway, Allura started to scream and weep out loud, not bothered about being heard.

"Oh God, why me? First my parents and now this. Why me? Is this some sort of test? Are you punishing me for some reason? What did I do to deserve all of this? What have I possibly done? I want to die! Just kill me now! Take me to my mum and dad, please. Anything is better than what I'm going through right now. Please just take me away, a million miles away from this horrible earth. Take me away!"

Allura couldn't stop thinking of her parents. She especially thought about her mum and yearned for a reassuring motherly hug. "Oh Mum, I wish you could just appear right now and give me one of your long, warm hugs that made me forget about the whole world. I need you, Mum. I miss you."

When she found herself crying uncontrollably, Allura decided to force herself up and made her way to the bathroom, where she spent the next ten minutes sitting on the edge of the bathtub, sobbing in remorse. Hands still wobbly, Allura decided to ignore Ahmed's request not to freshen up or shower. *What's done is done*, she thought to herself. Allura switched on the cold shower and slid her naked body under the shower head. It felt like she was cleaning her body of dirt and sin. The running cold water was therapeutic; by the time she was done, Allura started to feel the senses in her body coming back again.

As she walked out of the bathroom, she checked the cell phone. Ahmed had called her eight times.

"Ahmed, where are you? I'm sorry I missed your calls. I was in the shower."

"Didn't I say no shower? God damn it, Allura, you are stubborn! I'm downstairs. Can you come down?"

"Why don't you come up?"

"I'm not allowed upstairs. You come down. We'll sit somewhere private."

"I'll be there in five minutes."

Allura slipped on her loose-looking, masculine sweatpants, oversized t-shirt, and went down to meet Ahmed.

The second she spotted him standing by the hotel reception she limped as fast as she could towards him and threw herself at him. Hugging him tightly, Allura broke down in tears. Ahmed hugged her back, fiercely protective, as he kept whispering words of reassurance in her ear. "It's OK, I'm here now. Relax, shush now. It's OK, Allura. Try to calm down. Let's talk."

The receptionist noticed how upset Allura was and decided to give the two of them some space. Luckily it was low season, there were no customers by the reception area during that time. After a long hug, Ahmed held Allura's hand and suggested they go sit by the pool. The weather was breezy at that point, and he wanted Allura to breathe some fresh air.

"Ahmed, what do I do now? What do I tell my aunt? I don't get how this happened to me or who did this to me!"

"Allura, don't worry about your aunt now. I will speak with her. Now focus, please. Where were you? What was the last thing you remember? Do you recall anything about how you ended up limping like this?"

"I remember dancing with a friend till another person came and stood with us. It was just then that my friend Moe left and passed out on a couch. He didn't seem to be feeling too well."

"Slept on the couch? Was he high, drunk, or just tired? How well do you know that person?"

"Moe? Moe's a sweetheart. He's totally innocent, I assure you that much! He's with me at school, and I think he was just tired. You've met him once. He's that patient's grandson, remember?"

"Oh yeah, him. Yeah, I remember. Was he drunk, though?"

"He didn't drink much. I've been to a party with Moe before, and he drank triple that amount and was still sober!"

"How about you? How much did you have to drink?"

"I didn't drink too much at all, just a beer and two margaritas, but the second one I hardly finished. I remember feeling sick right after sipping the second margarita."

"Did you throw up?"

"I don't remember. I only remember dancing with that guy, Loay, and sipping my margarita. I don't remember anything beyond that."

"How are you feeling right now?"

"Awful!" answered Allura as tears started to roll down her cheeks again.

"I mean physically, how does your body feel?"

"I have a horrible migraine, my speech is slurred – as you might have noticed, my left leg hurts, my body is bruised, and I'm burning with aches and pains. I can hardly keep my balance."

"You mentioned that you were dancing with a guy called Loay. How well do you know him, and who is he exactly?"

"I don't know him at all. Now that I think of it, I remember Moe was uncomfortable about him being around. He kept telling me that he was hitting on me, and when he fell asleep by the couch, Loay wouldn't leave my side. He insisted on offering me a drink and dancing close by."

"So he was the one who offered you that margarita? Did he get Moe's drink too?"

"Yes, he got us both drinks and joined us on the dance floor till Moe excused himself and made his way towards the couch."

"Allura, darling, by the sound of things, that guy spiked your drink – probably both your drinks. This explains Moe's passing out episode and why you were knocked out and can't remember anything. Listen, I need you to describe where this party is. I'm going over there now to go speak to that bastard Loay. In the meantime, I need you to go back into your room and wait for me."

"I don't want to be left alone. I feel like I may do something foolish to myself."

"You won't do anything to yourself, Allura. Man up, woman! You're a strong girl. Please stop these shallow submissive ideas. You still have a whole lifetime ahead of you, and what happened was not your fault at all. Now, we'll worry about that later. I need to meet with that kid Loay for now. Stay put, OK? Go back up to your room, please. I promise I won't be late."

"He's no kid; he's about your age."

"Hmm, interesting, even better. I can't wait to beat the living hell out of him then. Now please go up, and keep this phone with you."

"It's running out of battery!"

Ahmed, luckily, had an extra charger with him.

After comforting Allura, Ahmed made his way to the beach house. He could feel his anger pulsating dangerously through his blood. It was going to take a lot of willpower not to rip Loay limb from limb.

As he drew closer, Ahmed could hear a roar of laughter and music drift across the breeze. The light atmosphere was a sharp contrast to his dark mood.

Ahmed made his way to the front door with gravel crunching under his shoes. Then he threw the door open, startling several partygoers.

"Loay! Loay! Where are you, you bastard? Adel! Where's Adel?" he bellowed, causing the music to grind to a halt.

"Dude, what's wrong? Chill out, man." A partygoer tried tentatively to approach the raving man tentatively.

"Don't touch me! Where's Adel? Loay!"

"Yo, man! Chill! I'm Adel. What's wrong?" asked Adel as he approached the angry visitor.

Ahmed growled and grabbed his collar. "How could you let that happen to her?"

"What? What happened? To who?"

"Don't mess with me! I'm talking about Allura! You let that animal hurt her in your own home!"

"What? What's going on? Look, let's go somewhere private, OK? I don't think Allura will appreciate you yelling about her private business like this."

"Fine." Ahmed shoved Adel in front of him. The curious crowd parted silently.

Adel led him to a secluded study.

"Start from the beginning. What happened to Allura?" Adel asked, shutting the door firmly.

"Allura has been raped. She kept mentioning some guy called Loay who gave her a drink that caused her to black out."

Adel was shocked. "Loay? Are you sure?"

"Yeah." Ahmed regarded the pale man in front of him suspiciously.

"Where is he? Bring him here now!"

"OK, OK, lemme see if I can find him," Adel said as he dialled his friend. "Yo, Loay, you still here, man? Can you come to the study, the one on the ground floor by the pool? OK, see you soon."

Adel looked up in sudden realisation. "Where's Moe, though? He was with Allura all day! He would know what went on."

Ahmed shrugged. "I don't know. Allura mentioned dancing with him before Loay handed them their drinks. If he was drugged too, he may need medical attention. Tell your friends to look for him, and while you're at it, get me Allura's belongings, her bag, phone, whatever you can find."

Adel fired off a mass text. He was rather fond of Moe and didn't want anything to happen to him. He soon received an update: they had found the unconscious teenager and were taking him to the hospital. He then phoned Anna, asking her to look for Allura's bag and bring it to the study.

"Hey Adel, can I come in?" Loay asked, as he reluctantly entered the room.

"Yeah, come in, man."

As soon as Loay entered the room, Ahmed slammed him into a wall.

"Hey! What gives? Who is this freak? Get the hell off of me!"

"Is that what Allura said when you raped her?" Ahmed roared, punching him repeatedly.

"What? Allura? Rape?"

"Don't mess with me! She said you gave her a drugged drink!" Ahmed's knuckles were blood splattered.

"Get off of me! Adel! Help! Do something, man!"

Adel shook his head sadly. "No, man, this is justice. You're lucky we're not calling the police."

"Are you fucking kidding me right now?" Loay snarled. "I'll call them myself!"

"You do that, and I'll tell them about your illegal party distribution business," Adel threatened.

"You double-faced motherfucker! You traitor! After all I've done for you!" Loay attempted to lunge at his former friend but was blocked by the furious doctor.

"We're not done yet! What did you put in their drinks?" Ahmed said, slamming Loay into the floor.

"Fuck you. I'm not saying shit."

Loay's once-handsome features had twisted into something vile and corrupted. Spitting out a wad of blood, he staggered to his feet.

Just then, Anna had walked into the room with Allura's belongings in hand. "What the hell! What is going on in here?"

Snatching Allura's things, Adel yelled at Anna, asking her to leave the room immediately before things got uglier.

"Oh no, you don't! You're not going anywhere! What. Did. You. Put. In. Their. Drinks?" Ahmed asked again, shaking Loay like a rag doll.

"OK, OK, OK, some sleeping pills or something I found in Adel's bathroom cabinet! Now get the hell off of me!"

Adel paled even further. "Oh shit, we gotta get them both to the hospital now. Those are some heavy-duty pills."

Ahmed glanced at him. "Do you know what they are?"

"No, but my parents said they're only supposed to take half a pill. If Moe took a higher dose..." Adel rushed out, shouting for someone to tell him which hospital his friend had been taken to.

"Oh no, you don't. We're not done," Ahmed said as he spied Loay trying to sneak out.

Grabbing the broken man, Ahmed punched him several more times.

"You don't see Allura again, you don't speak to her, and you don't even think of her. If you do, I'll know, and I'll finish what I started," he growled before dropping the blond man unceremoniously onto the Persian rug.

Approaching the door, Ahmed walked back to where Loay lay face up and spat on him.

"For the record, you haven't seen the last of me yet."

Stepping over him, Ahmed rushed out to get back to Allura. She needed to get to an emergency room.

Chapter 16

Flashbacks

On arrival to the emergency room that night, Allura was ushered to a private, quiet, comfortable area where a full medical examination was conducted. Her consent was obtained before beginning the history and during each phase of the physical examination and collection of evidence. An explanation of each step of the examination process was conducted, allowing her to recite details about the incident as far as she could remember.

Ahmed made sure to inform Nahed about what had happened in detail so that she could offer Allura emotional support throughout the whole process. Taken aback, Nahed rushed to the hospital the minute they hung up, arriving in record time.

Several days after the incident, Ahmed pulled some strings to transfer Allura to one of the finest hospitals in Cairo, where she received some of the best medical treatments, including gynaecology follow-ups and professional counselling.

Not long after, Allura requested that she continue her counselling sessions with Ahmed, despite him not being specialised to deal with her type of case. He just made her feel more comfortable.

Allura was diagnosed with post-traumatic stress disorder and continued to work with Ahmed to address what had happened to her that night. Ahmed was honest with Allura, explaining that he would take on the responsibility as a mere confidant rather than as a psychologist. He did, however, read up about the matter.

After spending several days in the hospital, Moe was discharged in the care of his parents, who forbade him from ever hanging out with Adel and his friends again. That suited him just fine; Moe had partied enough to last him till after university. He tried to reach out to Allura, but each attempt was shot down. Finally, he gave up and watched her sadly from a distance.

As news of his humiliating treatment at the hands of Ahmed spread, Loay found his reputation diminishing by the day. People who had once been frightened or wary of him became emboldened enough to challenge him or disregard his threats. In a desperate bid to salvage whatever remained from his reputation, Loay sold off his assets and left on the first plane out of Egypt. Despite several attempts by Ahmed to try to find Loay and get justice for Allura, no one knew of his exact whereabouts.

A year had passed since Allura was violated physically, mentally and spiritually. She got repeated flashbacks and nightmares; everything seemed to trigger her. She also became incredibly withdrawn, not speaking to anyone except her aunt, Ahmed, and Bassel. Her schoolwork suffered, and she barely managed to receive her diploma.

Allura and Ahmed had grown much closer since that night, but she was too ashamed to let whatever shred of hope she had blossom into affection. In the meantime, Bassel stood by Allura through everything, making sure to stay in constant contact through texts, Facebook messages, e-mails and even the odd Skype call.

***

Dear Bassel,

My life has changed. Nothing seems normal anymore, I don't seem normal. I feel uncomfortable in my own skin. Sometimes I even feel dirty! I don't feel like doing anything anymore, not even going to school or university or having fun with my friends.

139

Ahmed says all those feelings are just temporary. I hope so. I'm also on medication, and I think it's helping, but sometimes the side effects just make me feel so drained.

I've even suddenly become scared of doing stupid things, like walking down a street. Everyone's a potential attacker, and it's so draining to be so scared all the time.

Anyway, enough about my drama. How have you been? How's Pat doing? Hope you guys are happy together; you really deserve a wonderful life, Bassel!

Take care, hon. Miss you.
Love always, Allura

*****

My lovely Allura,

Words can't describe what I feel right now. It's so horrible what's happened to you, and I wish I were there to support you in person.

Allura, don't ever underestimate yourself, or feel dirty. Don't believe any of those horrendous ideas and thoughts. What happened to you was not your fault. You were drugged! I know it feels like every day's a struggle, but at least you're still alive and moving on, no matter how slowly. I'm sure Ahmed is a great guy and knows exactly what he's doing. Let him help you and stop those negative thoughts. Please!

You're now in university, the perfect place to reinvent yourself and discover your true passion. Are you still planning to major in business administration? Do they happen to have any design courses there? I remember you were very passionate about design!

Patricia is great. It's been over a year now, and we're still going strong! I even think she's the one. Anyway, we'll see how it goes. I'm hoping to visit Egypt by Christmas, which is when I'll ask her to come along. If she agrees, I'll definitely introduce you to her. I'm sure you two will get along. She actually reminds me of you quite a lot!

Take care, Allura.
All my love,
Bassel

***

When Allura first read that e-mail, she mulled over Bassel's question. Did she still want to major in business management? She had already started taking some classes in business and mass communications, which she enjoyed studying tremendously. In any case, she was still a freshman, and there was still time to choose her major.

After everything that had happened to her, Allura's decision to study abroad was deferred. She preferred to stay with her aunt in Cairo, which is where she studied, at the American University in Cairo.

Making her way to the patio, Allura sat down and observed her aunt twirl her cigarette around as though it were a smoking baton. Classical French music played softly in the background. She was gazing at the beauty surrounding her in her personal haven.

"You know, this is one of my favourite rooms in the house. I never get bored watching the scenery," Nahed said, glancing at her quiet companion. "Are you meeting with Dr Ahmed again today?"

"Yeah."

"Allura, lately you've been overly subdued, and I completely understand why. What you've been going through is daunting enough for any ordinary adult to take on. However, you need to spill things out every once in a while. I guess what I'm just trying to say is that I'm here for you if you'd like to open up about things."

"I know, Aunt Nahed."

"Is there something I do wrong? Is there something you need me to do? Can I help in any way?"

Allura interrupted. "Stop, Auntie. You're doing just fine, and I love you just the way you are. I just prefer to speak to you about other things, I guess. I hope that's all right with you."

"Anything is OK with me, just as long as you take good care of yourself. Now, change of topic. Since I'm privileged enough to have this conversation with you right now, what have you decided to major in?"

"Well, I've been wondering about the same thing. I am not sure. I was thinking of taking different classes this year and seeing where my passion really lies."

"That's very wise. Once you're a sophomore you can decide what it is you want to major in. Take your time. See what it is you enjoy studying and envision enjoying as a career."

Allura nodded.

"And how are things going with your shrink friend?" teased Nahed.

The teenager blushed.

"Oh, come now! I've certainly noticed the way you both look at each other. I may be old, but I'm not absent-minded. Mark my words, there's something special blossoming between you two," she teased, pointing the cigarette at her great-niece.

Allura stood up. "He's very dear to me, but I don't think I could ever be with a man again."

"Nonsense child! Never say never. What's important for now is that he seems to be a tremendous help and support for you." Nahed reclined back into the wicker chair.

Allura's phone rang right then. It was Ahmed. He was in front of the house waiting for her in his car. While Allura was speaking to him, Nahed suggested he come over for a quick drink.

"Actually, give me that phone," proposed Nahed as she pulled the phone away from Allura's ear playfully.

"Ahmed, it's been a while! Do you mind parking your car and blessing us with a short visit to our home? I'd love to see you for a few minutes."

"Sure, Aunt Nahed, I'll park and be right up," answered Ahmed suspiciously.

As he parked his car, he wondered why Nahed would ask to see him on such short notice. He figured she probably wanted to be updated on Allura's status. Then again, if she wanted to learn more about how Allura was doing, she could have simply picked up the phone and asked. The sudden invite started to make him nervous.

Ahmed's hands were slightly shaky as he rang the doorbell. He had no idea what to expect. It felt like he was courting a female from her family's home – a feeling he had never experienced before. He was always too consumed with his studies and work to even think of dating.

Allura stood right next to Nahed with a timid yet warm smile as she opened the front door to the mansion.

"Welcome to our home, my dear. Come in, please!" said Nahed, while extending her arms to hug Ahmed. Her unconventionally warm welcome immediately set Ahmed's mind at ease. "Finally you bless us with a long overdue visit to our home."

"I'm so sorry. If I only had known you wanted to meet me, I would have stopped by without hesitation. But Allura never mentioned it to me."

Leading him to the backyard patio, Nahed turned to look at Ahmed as she spoke. "The weather is beautiful tonight. So what is it you'd like to drink? What can we offer you?"

She placed her finger on the button of a bell push that was conveniently located on a nearby side table. It was especially designed to call for assistance from the kitchen.

Ahmed was impressed with how beautiful the house was. He also spotted a bottle of red wine and a half-filled glass right in front of Nahed, which put his mind at ease even more. He thought to himself, *Her aunt must be buzzed or relaxed by now; I can definitely relax around her.*

"Thank you, Aunt Nahed. I am good for now. You have a beautiful house, by the way."

"Oh, that's very kind of you. It's inherited, and every masterpiece in here is carefully selected. I take pride in my belongings and take very good care of them. Would you like to have some wine with me?" she asked as she reached out for her glass.

"No, no thank you. I don't drink. But please, go ahead, do enjoy your wine."

As they were chatting, Nahed's long-time butler showed up. "Yes, madame, how can I help you?"

"Ahmed, I insist you eat and drink something. You are in my house for the very first time. I don't want you leaving here saying this old woman isn't hospitable. Now, what would you like to have? We have everything hot you can imagine and everything cold you can dream of. If we don't have what you want, we'll make sure we get it for you. Right, Osman?"

"Yes, madame, that is correct. Sir, what would you like to drink? We really do have everything."

"Well, if you insist. Do you have cappuccino?"

"Yes, sir, we certainly do. I shall bring it with brown and white sugar on the side to allow you to take your pick." As he was about to leave the room, Osman stood to see if he was needed further. "Any other requests, sir, madame and mademoiselle?"

"Thank you, Osman. That will be all for now," said Nahed.

"Yes, madame. Excuse me," said Osman with a nod of the head as he courteously made his way out of the patio, walking backwards as a sign of respect.

Ahmed was amazed at how genteel and quick the service was in Nahed's home. It almost felt like a five-star hotel.

As the butler left the room, Nahed started to speak to Ahmed about the different designs and colours Osman made in his cappuccinos. "You may get a smiley face, a flower, a heart or any other design, depending on what he makes of you," she explained as she swigged a mouthful of wine with relish.

"Wow, that's amazing! I do hope I left a positive impression on him. I was initially nervous to come to your home. Now, I'm nervous about what to expect in my cappuccino mug!"

Nahed and Allura laughed at Ahmed's apprehensive yet humorous facial expression and comment.

The atmosphere was laid back. Everyone was at ease. Allura started to feel relaxed again.

After a good one-hour conversation, which mostly involved Nahed speaking about how faithful her butler, chef and housemaids were, she paused.

"Wait a second; I've been extremely talkative tonight. It must be a combination of the fine wine I'm drinking and your long-awaited company, Ahmed. Now, don't let me keep you more than I already have. You two had better move on with your plans."

It wasn't the first encounter for the two. Nahed and Ahmed had met on a number of occasions at the hospital after Allura's rape case, but the time wasn't right to get properly acquainted. His presence that day broke the ice between the two and got Ahmed even more intrigued to learn more about Allura.

"I thoroughly enjoyed your company, Aunt Nahed. If it's all right with you and Allura, I'd love to swing by again some other time."

"You can drop by anytime. Now you two have a great time tonight. Where do you plan to go?"

"Well, it's up to Allura. Our usual outing would be to the social club or the clinic in the meditative garden. We occasionally go to a nearby café or the mall. It's always her choice, to be honest."

"How boring is that? Why don't you go for dinner or a movie? You're both very young. Enjoy your youth! It's not all about therapy, you know. Maybe it's time you both take the time off and do something different tonight!"

"You're right, Aunt Nahed. Ahmed, are you hungry? Fancy some sushi? I know just the place," suggested Allura as they were all getting up.

Allura was thinking the sushi restaurant was busy enough to hide them from prying eyes yet secluded enough for them to have a proper conversation.

"I wouldn't mind sushi at all!" smiled Ahmed as he quickly surveyed Allura from head to toe. "You look lovely, by the way."

Allura placed a quick kiss on her aunt's cheek before darting out. "I love you, Auntie Nahed."

"Oh, my precious Allura, I love you more, more and much, much more!"

Allura and Ahmed starred at one another, trying to hold back their laughter. It was evident that Nahed had a bit too much to drink that night.

As she watched them walk out of the doorway, Nahed sighed. "Oh Haitham, oh Sawsan, she's so strong. But I think it's time she finds someone to share her burden, don't you agree?" She poured some more wine into her glass as an answering breeze ruffled her hair.

While escorting Allura to his silver sedan parked outside the mansion, Ahmed asked: "So, how are you feeling today?"

"I'm all right, I think. I didn't have a nightmare last night."

"That's great progress! I told you that you'd get there. One step at a time, right?" he said with a smile.

Allura glanced around uncomfortably. The street seemed too crowded at that point.

"Hey, hey. Focus on me. Ignore everyone else. It's just you, me, and the car we're about to get into," Ahmed reassured her.

"OK..."

Satisfied, he settled in his car seat, stretching his long legs.

"So, how was your day today? Are you enjoying your university?" he asked with a friendly smile as he began to drive away.

"My aunt thinks we're dating," Allura blurted out, covering her mouth in mortification.

Ahmed blinked. "Talk about a sudden change of subject! Say what now?"

Allura groaned in embarrassment. "Auntie Nahed! She thinks there's some spark or something between us…" she trailed off uncertainly.

Ahmed cleared his throat, trying to make sense of what had just happened.

"Allura, you know I have, um, strong feelings for you. But as someone much older, and as your informal shrink, it would be unethical for me to pursue anything with you, especially given your mental state," he said slowly, gauging her reaction.

Allura's face fell. "My mental state?"

"Don't be sad! You're very precious to me, and I wouldn't want to do anything to jeopardise our relationship or all the progress you've made so far," said Ahmed, reaching out to her.

"It's OK. I'm damaged goods anyway, I guess. You should be with someone whole and pure."

"Allura! Don't you dare speak that way about yourself, whether in my presence or otherwise. You're a survivor, and that makes you perfect. Any man who's lucky enough to land you will spend the rest of his life worshipping you."

"I don't want to be worshipped! I just want to be whole again! I'm so sick of people seeing what they want to see or projecting things onto me."

As they arrived to the driveway in front of the restaurant, Allura snatched her handbag. "Please, take me back home. Otherwise, I'll catch a taxi or something…"

"Allura, don't be silly. Don't make a scene. We just got here!"

Ahmed felt his heart become heavier. It always felt as though they were taking one step forward and two steps back.

Pulling out of the driveway, Ahmed came to a decision. "Allura, could you ask your aunt if she could speak with me once I drop you back home, please?"

Chapter 17

Even Eagles Let Go

Nahed blinked in surprise when she found Allura back so soon.

"Allura! Is that you? How come you're back already?"

"I don't want to talk about it, Aunt Nahed," she said as she raced up to the stairway hysterically, heading straight to her room and banging the door behind her.

Just then, the butler came to inform Nahed that Dr Ahmed was waiting outside the doorway.

Nahed shrugged.

"Really? He wants to meet with me? Well, we mustn't keep the gentleman waiting. Don't just stand there. Show him in, Osman. Oh, and get us both some Turkish coffee, please…quickly!"

"Yes, madame, right away." The long-time butler retired to fetch the unexpected guest.

"Dr Ahmed Barakat," intoned the butler upon his return.

"Hello again, Aunt Nahed. I apologise about the unexpected sudden visit. I guess I'm lucky tonight. I get to see you twice in less than an hour's time," he said, as he greeted the formidable woman.

"Ahmed, what happened exactly? How come you two are back this soon? Why has Allura rushed up to her room like that crying? She seems really upset!"

"Well, we got into a bit of a tiff, which is exactly why I decided to come speak to you. First off, I want you to know that Allura praises the ground you walk on."

"There'll be none of that talk. Goodness! You'd think I was a queen or something. I ordered some Turkish coffee for the two of us, by the way. Just wanted to check whether that's all right with you before you go on to talk."

"Turkish coffee sounds brilliant, thank you."

Settling down, Nahed turned a sharp gaze at the young man before her.

"Go on, spill. I've already gathered that this is not a social call, what's going on exactly?"

Ahmed fidgeted nervously.

"Allura's a remarkable young lady…"

"Yes. Tell me something I don't know already."

"Well—"

Nahed interrupted him.

"Look, you seem like a pleasant young man, and God knows astronauts from space could see just how deep your feelings are for each other. But Allura's only eighteen and still a freshman in university. She's also still recovering from that horrendous rape experience. With all honesty, I don't think she's ready to date, not you, and not any other man who may interest her."

"I agree, she still needs time to fully heal. And yes, given that I am her therapist, even though it's not my speciality, there's a huge conflict of interest if I were to pursue her romantically right now," said Ahmed. "But with your blessings and Allura's consent, I'd like to try a romantic relationship with her – when the time's right, of course."

Nahed narrowed her eyes. "I'm not entirely comfortable with the idea. I'd like Allura to focus on getting her life together first, and that requires time, a lot of time."

"I completely agree," reassured Ahmed. "But what I meant to say is—"

Adamant to change the topic, Nahed said: "Good, glad we're in agreement. Now that's settled, I insist you stay for dinner."

Days passed after Ahmed and Nahed's late-night conversation. When she felt Allura was approachable and calmer, Nahed decided to relay the discussion to her over breakfast, resulting in a much-needed heartfelt conversation.

"Allura, you know I've never liked to pressure you in any way, which is why I left you for a few days to calm down. What was wrong with you exactly when you barged in the house crying like that the other day?" asked Nahed inquisitively.

"I'm sorry Aunt Nahed, I haven't been myself lately, as you may have realised…Ahmed and I had a brief conversation about our relationship, and I…well, I was turned down by him, basically. It hurt, given that—" She sighed. "Well, given that he's about the closest person to my heart these days – other than you, of course."

Nahed smiled gracefully.

"My sweet child, Allura, what if I tell you that Ahmed is head over heels for you? Which is exactly why he came to meet me that same evening."

"Really? Well, he did say that he wanted to speak with you, but I thought it was because I was acting out that way!"

After listening attentively to what Nahed had to say about Ahmed's intentions, the teenager was keen on starting a romantic relationship as soon as possible, terrified of the prospect that Ahmed might decide he'd like to date or marry someone else.

Nahed advised caution, noting that Allura still had her whole life ahead of her, full of experiences waiting to be discovered. The discussion soon escalated into a heated argument, and both women retreated before something terrible was said. Nahed's growing concern about Allura's welfare and the impact the relationship may have had on her mental state caused the elderly woman to reach out yet again to her stalwart friend.

After hearing the whole story from Nahed, Dr Alaa commented: "Let her go."

"Are you serious? After all my blabbing, that's all you can come up with? Three words?"

"My dearest Nahed, let me tell you a story. Do you know what an eagle does with its baby eaglet? Not long after it's born, while teaching it to fly, the mother eagle will take her baby high above the clouds. The little bird, sitting on his mother's back and looking around, thinks to himself how beautiful and comforting the view is from up there. Just then, while the baby bird feels secure and happy with its mother, the eagle lets go of its baby and darts out from underneath, leaving the eaglet stranded in mid-air. The little bird flaps its wings as hard as it can, but they will not give him any traction. He falls at an alarming rate towards rock bottom. The little bird shuts its tiny eyes in despair, thinking it's the end of him. Just when the baby is ready to hit the ground, his mother appears once again and bears her baby on her wing."

"That's a tragic story, Alaa! Why are you telling me this? That's a horrible thing to do to a baby, especially coming from a mother," sighed Nahed.

"It's not, Nahed. It's actually the right thing to do, and this is a true story of how the mother eagle teaches its child to survive. There is no way to do that other than to toughen up her eaglet and let it try, again and again. You've got to let her try. You told her how you feel already. Now it's really up to her to make things either work or not."

"But I can foresee a problem with her getting herself involved so early. Don't my years of experience and my maturity level have any say in this? I've lived long enough to have intuitions and to sense danger before it knocks on my door."

"Your feelings are perfectly normal, and you have the right to feel concerned given all that's happened. But you have no right to impose your state of mind on Allura. Besides, Nahed, please do not forget how sensitive things are for her right now, given her circumstances."

"Exactly, and for that same reason, I won't be able to stomach seeing her hurt like that again. All this time I've been following your advice and letting her go. I was too loose, to the extent that I actually dug her grave with my own hands. Look at what's happened to her due to my looseness. She got raped! Yeah, let her go. Right, Alaa! Sure!"

"What happened was nowhere near your fault. It was pure bad luck. Nahed, too much analysis leads to paralysis! You've got to stop thinking ahead so much. What's the worst that could happen? If her heart breaks, she'll just learn from it and move on like the rest of the human race! Besides, it's not like they're getting married tomorrow. The man simply expressed his serious intentions to court her in the future, which is a decent and rare thing to do; I personally respect him for it. Nahed, I really think you're blowing this out of proportion!"

"See, that's where I have a problem. I don't think Allura can take any more pressure in her life. She's been through a lot. Her parents' passing away was a huge blow on its own. She's just not living the way a normal girl her age should live. She hasn't been very lucky with anything in her life, and I feel she's bottling up a lot more than I'm aware of. She's going through a lot and not telling me half of it because she doesn't want to hurt me. Allura is a lovely soul..." said Nahed tearfully.

"I still don't get where the problem is."

"The problem is, well, she hardly has any friends, other than this guy, Bassel, who lives across the globe from her and this Dr Ahmed, who's eager to tie her down. Where's her chance to explore her potential and life in general? Where's her freedom to make choices?"

"You're talking from the perspective of an overprotective mother who wants to nurture and shelter her child forever, but Allura is no baby. She's a fine young lady who is quite charismatic, from what I hear about her. She'll be fine, Nahed. After everything that's happened to her, Allura has most definitely developed thick skin. It's actually you I'm worried about right now. You're far too emotional about this whole thing. Just relax; it'll all work out fine at the end. Even if things don't work out the way you envision them, she'll bounce back in no time, trust me."

Chapter 18

Graduation Day

The huge box sat innocently on the desk in her room, still bearing the stamps of a rushed delivery. It had arrived the night before, with strict instructions to only be opened in the morning. Allura grinned as she ripped it open, squealing in delight at the large teddy bear that emerged, clutching flowers in one hand, and a framed photograph of her and Bassel in the other.

There was also a small card attached to the flowers.

***

"My beautiful Allura, how I wish I were with you on your graduation day. But since I'm not, I thought of sending you the three most precious things: a graduation bear that will be by your side at all times when I am not; a bouquet of flowers symbolising how beautiful you are in my eyes; and a picture to remind you of how close we'll always be in heart and soul. I've always got your back. Never forget that. Enjoy your big day, princess."

***

Allura teared up at the thoughtful message. Checking the time, she realised that it was probably too late in the evening to phone Bassel. Grabbing her phone, she dashed off a thank-you message.

***

***

A few minutes later, her mobile phone rang.

"Hey, you! I was going to call you, but I thought you'd be sleeping! How are you? Thank you for the beautiful gifts, Bassel. I have no idea how you managed to send such beautiful, fresh flowers all that way!"

"You're very welcome. So, how are you feeling this fine graduation morning?" said Bassel, laughing.

"I'm so excited! I can't wait to get out and put everything I've learnt to the test! Plus, I'm probably going to start planning for the wedding. I mean, we haven't set a date yet, but you know me. I always like to be prepared."

"Are you sure that you want to get married that fast? I mean, you're still so young. Don't you want to experience life first before settling down?"

"Ugh, you sound like my aunt now!"

"Well, your aunt is wise and has experience on her side. Maybe you should listen to her, every now and then – especially, after all you've been through."

"Ahmed is great to me, Bassel. He's stood by me through thick and thin, so what better person than him to spend the rest of my life with? I really feel this is the right thing to do. Plus, I want to start a family of my own. Ever since Mum and Dad died, I've felt so alone. Having a family would help fill that void."

"See, that's what I was worried about. I'm not sure you love this guy enough to marry him. You just love the idea of him being around you all the time and want to rush into having your own family. Don't let what happened to your mum and dad rush you into starting a family this young. You're only twenty-one years old. Be true to yourself, Allura!"

"Bassel, I've known him for long enough to know what I'm doing. Don't worry about me, please. Speaking of which, when are you and Pat tying the knot?"

"We're not. We broke up."

"Huh? When exactly did this happen? How come you never told me about this before?"

"She was complaining that I was travelling too much, but that's my career. It's my life. If she can't handle what I do, then there's no way we can continue to see one another. Besides, I wasn't about to marry her that fast anyway. We were happily dating. I have a long way ahead of me before I even think of going down the lane."

"But I thought you felt that she was the one?"

"I did feel that way, but that doesn't mean marrying her! I was thinking if things continued to be serious between us, she could possibly move in with me, but marriage. Nah! Nowhere close…"

"I'm sorry to hear that. You guys seemed great together. Hopefully, things will work out, or else you'll find someone else that makes you just as happy as Pat did."

"Thanks. Well yeah, it was rough when we first broke up, but that was a while ago. I'm OK now, focusing on getting back into the game. I'm only twenty-two, Allura. Life still awaits me!"

"What do you mean by getting back into the game?"

"Remember my shoulder injury? When I said that my swimming career might be over? I spoke to my coach again, and he's got me on this intense training programme. We're hoping I'll be in good shape for the US National Championships next year."

"Oh wow, well good luck. But in case that doesn't work out, have you got a Plan B or something?"

"You're always looking out for me," said Bassel with a chuckle. "Nope, no Plan B for me. I'm focusing on my sports career for now. Once I'm sure that's over, I'll figure something else out. I like to take things one day at a time."

"It's not good to put all your eggs in one basket, Bassel. Why don't you go back to university, take a couple of classes, and see if there's something interesting for you? Maybe you can get a degree in sports rehab or something…"

"I'll think about it when the time comes. Anyway, it's getting late, and I'm sure your aunt's got a million things planned for you before your ceremony today. Give her my regards, and we'll catch up later."

"OK, sure. Thanks again for the gorgeous teddy bear and for calling me. Talk soon, take care!"

Allura wondered what it would be like if Bassel were in Cairo with her once again. Would that bond still remain if they were both in the same city? Would things be different? What if they had drifted apart? That would have devastated her.

Her thoughts were suddenly interrupted. "Allura! Are you awake, dear? It's time for breakfast!"

"Coming, Auntie Nahed! I'll be there in a few minutes!"

"All right, sweetie. Catch up with me in the garden. It's such a lovely, sunny day out."

"OK, Auntie, I'm coming. Just give me a few minutes!"

Allura bounded to the wardrobe, throwing the elaborately curved door open, and reached in for her graduation cap and gown. Gently running her fingers through the material, she smiled to herself. It had been a long, hard road, but she had finally made it. She was going to walk onto that stage and accept her degree, with honours, in business administration.

The young woman marvelled at just how fast time had passed. It seemed like just yesterday she was debating what to major in. Now, countless classes, projects and exams later, she was going to head out into the real world and show everyone just what a force she could be.

It had been hard being separated from Ahmed for so long. He had travelled to London for further studies during Allura's sophomore year. They stayed in touch through video calls, e-mails, texts and even the odd visit by Ahmed. His visits were always short, though, which made their yearning grow with each encounter. Talk eventually turned to marriage, and while they couldn't wait to start the rest of their lives together, both agreed that they should hold off until after Allura graduated and Ahmed returned permanently to Cairo.

Allura's thoughts returned to the present abruptly when Osman knocked on her door, reminding her that Nahed was still waiting. She made her way to the courtyard and settled down in the white wicker chair next to Nahed.

"So, have you thought about what you'd like to do now?" Nahed asked in trepidation.

"Well, along with preparing for my future wedding, I'm obviously planning to look for a job. I'm not sure if I want to stay in Cairo, though. Maybe I'll look for something back in Abu Dhabi. I really miss being there. Or maybe abroad? At the same time, I don't want to be so far away from Ahmed. Maybe I'll go to London and see if there's anything for me there," she replied, taking a sip of coffee.

"Hmm. Well, you know I'd hate to see you go. You've practically become my daughter, and while I know I'll never be able to replace your mother—"

"Auntie Nahed, you know how fond I am of you. You've been there for me through everything, and I don't know how I'll ever be able to repay you."

"The best way to repay me is by having a rich, fulfilling life, and watching out for yourself as best as you can, regardless of where you decide to end up. Promise?"

"Promise," Allura responded, wrapping her pinkie around her aunt's finger.

The ceremony was long but exhilarating. Everywhere Allura looked, cameras were flashing, families were beaming and fellow students were chattering elatedly.

When her name was called out, Allura clutched the locket containing her parents' photographs before ascending the stage to accept her diploma and congratulations from the smiling dean. Heading back to her seat, she couldn't contain the broad grin that stretched across her face upon spotting her old neighbours – Flavio and Lucy, who were seated next to Aunt Nahed and Gladdis. Her eyes widened upon spotting an unexpected addition – Ahmed was there, beaming proudly and clutching a beautiful bouquet.

Once the ceremony ended, Allura made a beeline to the group, hurling herself into Flavio's arms for a tight hug before turning to hug everyone else.

"I am very proud of you, my princess. You look stunning, and you will always have a special place in my heart," whispered Nahed in Allura's ears as they hugged, causing the younger woman to clutch her even tighter.

Letting go, she turned to the love of her life, wiping away a few stray tears as she smiled in disbelief. "Is that really you? Or am I dreaming?"

"It's me all right, in the flesh," answered Ahmed with a huge grin on his face. "Did you honestly think I would miss this day? I know how special this is for you, and to be honest, I was pretty excited to see you in your graduation robe. You made it!"

The emotional moment was broken by the sound of Nahed clapping her hands. "Ladies and gentlemen! Now that the stuffy part is over, it's time to celebrate! Cocktails and champagne are waiting back at the house. Let's go!"

Nahed had been preparing for the happy evening for the past week. The backyard patio was filled with exquisite carnation flowers, candles and a huge banner suspended between two trees, which read 'Congratulations, Allura, you did it!'

The family chef had spent the entire day working on his famous barbecue, and a live band performed upbeat music all night long. Champagne bottles and assorted appetisers were lined up on the bar for the guests to indulge in.

"Aunt Nahed, this is amazing, thank you!"

"You're most welcome, my dear. This is a most special occasion, after all. How many times do we get to celebrate your university graduation?" Nahed replied, clutching Allura's hand warmly.

Turning to the guests assembled before them, Nahed reached for a nearby champagne bottle.

"Flavio, as a dear friend of Allura's, why don't you do the honours and open the first bottle of the evening?"

"Avec plaisir, madame," said Flavio, who opened the bottle with a flourish before pouring its contents into the assembled glasses.

"Thank you, Flavio. I don't drink." Ahmed declined the offered glass with an upturned hand.

Turning to Allura, Ahmed added: "It's your special day, and I know you like to have a drink every now and again, but you know I don't like alcohol. Forgive me if I seem rude. I'll just have a juice or something."

"Oh, sure, no worries!" Allura said, glancing at her aunt in embarrassment.

Nahed was discreetly fuming. She didn't care that Ahmed didn't condone the drinking of alcohol, but he should have pulled her aside at the start of the party so such an embarrassing scene wouldn't occur in front of all her guests. "I'm sure we can find a refreshing glass of juice for you. Any preferences?"

"Lemonade with mint, if you have some, please."

"Very well." Nahed snapped her fingers at a nearby waiter, who hurried to fulfil the request.

"Thank you, Nahed. I'm sorry again if I disturbed the mood," said Ahmed.

"Nonsense. Ah, here we go," she said subtly, handing over the tall glass.

"OK, everyone. Now that we're ready, let's toast to Allura and her great success!"

"To Allura!" chanted everybody in one go.

"Thank you, everyone, and thank you for being here tonight to share this special day with me. Please, help yourselves to some of our chef's delicious food before there's none left," Allura said jokingly. "OK, fellas, let's heat it up!" she added, nodding at the band, who immediately launched into an up-tempo beat.

The crowd cheered before dispersing into various corners.

"And who might you be, my dear? I know you are Allura's friend, but we were not properly introduced," commented Lucy as she walked towards Ahmed. She had just caught up with the rest of the group.

Ahmed laughed. "I apologise if I didn't properly introduce myself. I'm Ahmed, Allura's fiancé, and hopefully one day, very soon, her husband."

"He's not her fiancé yet. He proposed, and I agreed on the condition that Allura finishes her studies and finds a job," interrupted Nahed with some irritation.

Nahed wasn't quite sure what to make of Ahmed. She found him well-mannered and an overall pleasant person, yet there was something not quite right about him that she couldn't put her finger on.

"Well hey, once you're done drinking your juice, show me some of your dancing moves!" Lucy said in an attempt to diffuse the rising tension.

"It would be my pleasure." Ahmed grinned, offering his elbow after putting down his glass.

"Later, pals!" Lucy waved as they made their way to the dance floor.

Nahed reached out to Allura as she tenderly hugged her. "My dear, there's something I'd like to give you tonight."

"Auntie Nahed, you didn't have to! All of this is so much more than I expected."

"Now, this is no time for modesty. This is a grand occasion, and a grand occasion deserves a grand gift. Here," she said, handing her a small, gift-wrapped box.

"What is it?" asked Allura as she opened the small jewellery box.

Nahed had given Allura an enamel heart-shaped brooch made out of rubies, sapphires and yellow diamonds, engraved with Allura's name.

"Oh my God, this is so beautiful. But you didn't have to spend so much on me! You've done too much already," said Allura in astonishment.

"It's a simple token of my admiration and respect for you. I am very proud of whom you've become, and it is with pleasure that I give you this small token on your special day."

"Oh, is it time to give the gifts? Wait, let me get mine!" said Lucy, looking slightly dishevelled from keeping up with the band.

"Aunt Lucy! Not you too!"

"Of course, me too. Here," she said, handing over another box.

"What's up with the boxes today?" Allura said laughing as she opened the heart-shaped jewellery case. It was a personalised graduation bracelet with yellow and white gold charms.

"Thank you, Aunt Lucy and Uncle Flavio. I don't know what to say. This is far too much!" Allura got up and hugged Nahed, Lucy, and Flavio.

Aunt Gladdis then gave Allura an envelope. "I guess my present is slightly different," she said with a cheeky grin.

Allura gasped when she saw the amount within: "This is too much, Auntie Gladdis! I couldn't accept—"

"Don't be silly child. You've accepted two expensive gifts already. I'm just giving you cash instead. I figured you're just like me – you prefer to buy your own thing instead of being saddled with tacky gifts," Gladdis said with a cheeky wink.

"Oh, Aunt Gladdis, you've always been very practical. Thank you so much," said Allura, hugging the older woman. "But the gifts aren't tacky. They're beautiful," she added with a giggle.

"Now it's my turn. Save the best for the last, as they say," said Ahmed.

Nahed shot him a dark glare, not appreciating the arrogant tone.

As Ahmed approached Allura, he got down on one knee and gently grasped her hand.

"Allura, would you make me the happiest man in the world by giving me the honour of calling you my wife? Will you marry me?" he asked, holding up a sparkling diamond ring.

The room grew still. Even the band and the busy waiters stopped their activities.

Allura swallowed heavily. They had talked about marriage, but she didn't think that Ahmed would formally propose during her graduation celebration, at least not propose publicly. Allura glanced at her aunt as though seeking guidance.

"This is your special night, Allura, but this is also a big step for you both. Just know that I'll support you, whatever you decide," Nahed said encouragingly. There would be time later to give Ahmed a piece of her mind for that outrageous stunt.

Taking a steadying breath, Allura nodded.

"Yes, yes, I will marry you!"

Ahmed let out an undignified whoop before jumping to his feet and sliding the ring onto her finger.

"You've made me so happy, Allura. I promise I'll take care of you for the rest of our lives."

Nahed approached to congratulate the happy couple. As she drew Ahmed close, she whispered: "Darling, may I remind you that it is part of our tradition to bring along your mother and father and to propose to me formally, which is when further details shall be discussed and decided."

"Yes, of course, Aunt Nahed. I completely understand that, and I will speak to Allura regarding arranging a meeting between the two families as soon as possible. My parents already know about my intentions tonight and are even willing to come over now, if you'd prefer."

"No, no, not tonight. I will expect them tomorrow or, at the most, the day after. Just let Allura know what time they plan to visit, so all the proper arrangements can be made."

"Yes, Aunt Nahed. Of course. Now, if you'll excuse us, I'd like to dance with my fiancée."

Ahmed led Allura onto the dance floor. Her diamond ring glittered under the strobe lights. As the band struck up a romantic ballad, he held her close as the world faded away. Allura sighed as she snuggled closer, hardly believing what a magical day it had been.

Chapter 19

The Family Feud

Ahmed passed on Nahed's request for a formal meeting between the families over dinner a few days later at his parents' home.

"Ahmed, dear, you must come over more often. We hardly see you anymore," remarked his mother.

"I'm sorry, Mother. But you know I've got such a busy schedule at the centre—"

"Shawki, why don't you lighten the poor boy's load?" she interrupted, turning to the man slurping soup beside her.

"Now, now, Rasha, he's a grown man. If he thinks the workload's too much, then he could come and see me himself."

"The workload's fine. Can we please forget about the workload?" Ahmed said irritably.

"That's no way to speak to your parents. You know we've got your best interests at heart," Rasha scolded.

Ahmed sighed. "Yes, Mother. I'm sorry. Can we please get back to talking about the meeting?"

"Ah, yes, with that girl's aunt. Tell me, who's the mystery girl you've proposed to? I mean, you simply come up to me one night and say you've met the woman of your dreams and want to propose to her with your grandmother's ring!"

Ahmed cleared his throat and took a sip of water.

Shawki was focused with reading the newspapers. He was always preoccupied with anything other than his son, unless it involved work. Ahmed had been forced to become responsible at a young age due to his father's eagerness to pass on the clinic to him someday. Growing up, he barely saw his parents. His childhood memories were mostly of various babysitters and neighbours looking after him. On most days, Rasha was barely home. During the mornings, she'd spend time in the women's club indulging in tea and coffee over long conversations with friends. In the evenings, she would accompany her husband to different business dinners or outings.

"Well, her name's Allura. She's twenty-one years old and just graduated from a business administration programme. She was born in London and lived most of her life in the United Arab Emirates but was forced to move to Egypt due to her parents' accident. She's from a good family, and she is very polite, well brought up and beautiful."

Intrigued by the story, Shawki put the newspapers aside. "What exactly happened to her parents?"

"Well, they were on their way to her farewell school party, since they had all decided to move to Egypt at the time. The car engine caught fire due to a leakage, and they unfortunately burned alive. She was only sixteen when this happened. Since then, she has lived in Egypt with her father's aunt."

"How awful!" gasped his mother.

"Yes, but she's so strong, Mother. She's overcome so much, and she's got such a bright future ahead of her. And I want to be there for her every step of the way."

His parents exchanged concerned looks.

"Son, we understand that you're in love with…Allura…but there's other factors you need to consider. You come from a prominent family. What would people think if you married someone who's practically a stranger?"

"Father, that's not fair. Since when have we really cared about what others think of us? Anyway, you know I could've just eloped with Allura. In spite of everything that's between us, I still respect you both as my parents and Nahed as Allura's guardian."

"Ahmed!" his mother cried in distress. "What do you mean by eloped? You make me sad with your inconsiderate words. After all those years of investing in your upbringing, that's the sort of appreciation you pay us back with? Don't push your luck now. Your father is just being realistic and is trying to get to the bottom of this!”

“Stop it. You’re being dramatic as always. Look, I’ve never really said anything, despite the fact that I’ve been practically raised by strangers and you’ve just trotted me out on account of your parties, like some sort of statue or prize. For once, can you please just think of my happiness and agree to meet with them?”

As Rasha was ready to answer back, Shawki held his hand up. “Rasha, wait, please. Son, I have no issues if she’s from a good family and is well brought up. I just need to ask about her family history a bit before you take this step. Don’t forget your legacy. You come from one of the richest and most refined families in Egypt.”

“Father, with all due respect, her family are probably way better than we are, and there’s no need to ask. I’ve made up my mind about marrying Allura. I just need you and Mother to be with me when I propose to her aunt formally.”

“Oh how nice, so you don’t even want us to check who you’re marrying? Given that you are one of the most eligible bachelors in Egypt, the least your father can do is ask about this girl’s background. We will never step foot into that house before we get a little more clarity on who she is exactly. Ahmed, you are Dr Shawki Barakat’s son. Please do not forget that!”

“Oh, please, just drop these ridiculous stereotypes already. Just let me know when you can go visit her aunt. And Mum, please, don’t refer to her as ‘this girl’ or ‘she’. Her name is ‘Allura’ and she will be my wife soon,” replied Ahmed in a tone almost as sarcastic as Rasha’s.

“What kind of name is Allura, anyway?” Rasha’s sarcasm was nothing new. Shawki himself tried to avoid arguing with her, he simply had no time to hear her whining and nagging about things.

Ahmed rolled his eyes. He knew his mother pretty well, she always had to have the last word. “Mother, I am going to try to stop arguing with you right now, because if this conversation prolongs, I will lose my temper!”

"Ahmed! I can't speak to you when you're this disrespectful. Please leave, now! We'll discuss this again when you've calmed down," his mother said sharply.

"Fine!" Ahmed slammed his hands onto the mahogany table, causing the cutlery to clink, before storming out of the house.

He was thinking to himself his life wasn't much different than that of Allura's as a single child. The only difference was that her parents were forced to leave her behind due to fate, and his, well, they chose to lead a selfish, pretentious lifestyle instead of spending quality time with their only child.

"Oh, Shawki, whatever are we going to do with him?"

Shawki tactfully patted his distraught wife's hand. "Don't worry, Rasha. I'll speak to him and straighten everything out."

A later day found both men sitting in Shawki's office, sipping a cup of coffee as they discussed a few things related to the centre. Soon, the conversation turned to Ahmed and his future bride.

"Son, I've asked around about your wife-to-be, and she seems to come from a fine background. Not only were her parents in good standing, but she's also received a substantial inheritance."

"Dad, I am not marrying Allura for her money. I have a lot of my own, thanks to our family business."

"I understand, Ahmed, but it wouldn't hurt to have some extra money in case of anything."

"I'm not some gold digger, Dad! Anyway, weren't you and Mum just telling me about acting according to my status in society?"

"That's different. Don't twist my words. No wonder you and your mother don't get along. You're quick to judge and equally dramatic."

"I'm nothing like her!"

"You will not disrespect her in my presence!" roared Shawki, startling his son into silence. Clearing his throat, he continued: "In any case, I've discussed it with your mother, and we're fine with meeting this girl's aunt and working out the details of your nuptials."

"Thank you, Father. And 'this' girl is called Allura." Ahmed exhaled in relief. "I'll call her right away and set everything up."

"That's fine, Ahmed. Oh, and congratulations in advance, by the way." With that, his father dismissed him.

"Yes, thank you, Father. I'll get back to you soon."

Ahmed hurried down the hallway, ear pressed firmly to his mobile phone. He didn't want to tempt fate by waiting too long to get the elders together.

Chapter 20

A Formal Proposal

Nahed sighed, taking in the tearful scene before her. While she had agreed to meet Ahmed's parents the next day, she had also lectured Allura on the importance of securing her career and not throwing away everything she had worked so hard on just for the sake of getting married and having children. That led to a heated argument, and both women retreated to lick their wounds.

"Allura, darling, you know I never meant to hurt you. You know I'm happy for you. I just don't want you to throw your life away for some man."

"He's not some man! He's the love of my life!" Allura's scream was muffled by the thick blanket.

"Oh, oh, you know I didn't mean it like that," Nahed said, patting the misshapen lump.

Allura's tearful eyes peeked out. "I miss them so much, Auntie Nahed. I always thought they'd be around when I got married and when I had babies—"

"When you became CEO of a big company, and for so many other achievements…I know, Allura. But I'm here, and you know I'll never leave you," Nahed said comfortingly.

Allura sniffled. "I know."

"Come now, dry your tears, and let's have a soothing cup of tea and put this ugly incident behind us. You must be bright-eyed for tomorrow's meeting, after all," Nahed suggested.

"OK."

"That's my girl! Now, young lady, go and freshen up. I'll be waiting in the veranda."

The soothing sounds of trees rustling in the breeze greeted Allura as she made her way to the table laden with china and snacks.

"Allura, honey, I know I promised I wouldn't speak about this subject anymore. But there's one thing I need to ask of you, if that's all right?"

"All right, Auntie," Allura said, accepting the proffered cup of tea.

"Allura, you know that your parents left you a sizeable inheritance, of which there's still quite a lot, and Ahmed earns a good salary at the centre. I'm concerned that you're throwing away a lot of opportunities with all that you've got."

"Auntie Nahed, with all due respect, I'm done talking about that topic, but since you insist on bringing it up all the time, I'll lay it out for you once and for all. My original plan was to pursue a career right after graduation; however, that was before I was formally engaged to be married. Now things have changed, and there's just no rush. I can take a year, maybe two, off, so Ahmed and I can settle into a married routine. Then, I'll look for a job or even open my own business."

"I just don't understand why Ahmed isn't encouraging you to start a career, after all his support for you during your university studies. He's seen your potential. Why wouldn't he encourage you to nurture it? Besides, prior to the proposal you were thinking of taking up a career in another country. Whatever happened to that thought?"

Allura sulked. She knew her aunt wasn't about to give up speaking about the same topic again. "Ahmed and I have already discussed this, and he doesn't like the idea of me tiring myself. He thinks I should stay home and receive the royal treatment. I'll just sit there, take care of myself, get pampered and be served all day long. I deserve the well-earned break!"

"You must be joking! Please don't tell me Ahmed is the controlling type?"

"He's not controlling. He simply cares for my well-being."

"Well, so do I!"

Allura stood up quickly, the chair screeching harshly on the stone paving.

"Auntie Nahed, I'm tired. Thank you for the tea. Like you said, it's best that I rest so I can be refreshed for our meeting with Ahmed's parents tomorrow. Please excuse me."

She left without waiting for her aunt's dismissal.

"That girl! Honestly. She can be so stubborn sometimes!" Nahed muttered crossly to herself as she reached out for a mini strawberry tart. "I just hope everything goes smoothly. God knows, she's had such a rough life already."

Back in her room, Allura was pacing agitatedly as she relayed what had happened to Ahmed.

"Your aunt cares for you, Allura. Take it with a good heart. But at the end of the day, it's up to you, sweetie. I never told you not to work. I just advised you to take some well-earned time off because you just graduated. You are more than welcome to work at the centre again if you'd like to."

"Oh, Ahmed, that is exactly why I'm marrying you. You're so sweet, and you genuinely care about me."

"Everything will be fine. You're just nervous about the meeting tomorrow. You know, I am too. I've had butterflies all day thinking about it!"

Allura giggled. "You have not."

"I have too," Ahmed responded teasingly.

"I just can't wait for everything to be over. Why isn't it tomorrow already? I could be planning our wedding!"

"Oh, had many fantasies about that, have you? Tell me some of your plans."

"Well, I'd like it to be a small ceremony, actually, with just our families and maybe a couple of selected friends. I'd love to be able to invite Bassel."

"You can invite anyone you'd like to. What about the venue?"

"If you don't mind, I'd like to have the reception on a Nile cruise, with just a few of our friends and family."

"That sounds like a great idea. What about the food?"

"We could have a proper five-course meal, and of course we'll have a beautiful wedding cake."

"The biggest and most stunning wedding cake in all of Cairo," Ahmed teased.

"I'm hanging up. You're too silly."

"All right, my love. But before you do, can you blow me a kiss?"

Allura complied.

Ahmed hooted. "What I would give to be there in person to receive such a sweet kiss from such a sweet woman."

"Good night, Casanova."

"Good night, light of my life."

The next morning, the house was filled with a restless energy as everyone bustled around, making sure everything was perfect for the distinguished guests. Nahed had left strict instructions for a three-course lunch to be prepared, along with coffee and light refreshments for later.

In the meantime, Allura and her aunt were at the beauty salon getting ready. It was important to give a good first impression for her future in-laws, after all. Returning home, they changed into suitable attire before retiring to the living room to wait for the Barakats.

"Oh, Auntie, I'm so nervous!" Allura said, playing with some strands of hair.

"Stop that! You'll ruin your beautiful hairdo. Take a deep breath. Everything will be just fine. In any case, nothing brings people together like good food!"

Allura's giggles turned to gasps as the doorbell rang.

"Remember, my dear, deep breaths," Nahed advised as they rose to greet their guests.

"Allura! You look absolutely ravishing. Hello, Aunt Nahed. It's a pleasure to meet you again. May I introduce you both to my parents, Shawki and Rasha?"

"I'm delighted to meet you both. Please sit down. Would you like some coffee or tea?" Nahed asked as they exchanged pleasantries.

"An espresso for me, please," said Rasha.

Once everyone had related their requests to the butler, talk turned to a range of topics before they came to the matter at hand.

"Well, now that we've gotten to know each other better, let's get down to the main purpose of our visit today," suggested Shawki.

"Very well," said Nahed.

Part of the discussion was with regards to where the couple would reside. The families settled on a newly furnished villa that Ahmed owned, located an hour away from where Nahed lived. They also agreed that the wedding party expenses would be settled by the groom. In case of a divorce or death, a sum of money was agreed upon as compensation for Allura, which is was what the Egyptians referred to as '*Moakhar Sadak*'.

"I think we've discussed everything in detail. Is there anything else you'd like from us or need to ask, Madame Nahed?" asked Shawki.

"Well, not from you as such. I'd like to hear more from the groom." Nahed turned to look at Ahmed with a demure smile. "We haven't heard much from you this evening, Ahmed. I hope you're not nervous around me?"

Ahmed balked. "Not at all, Aunt Nahed. I look forward to being a part of your family. Please don't hesitate to ask me anything."

"You know, Ahmed, you're an extremely smart young man, smart enough to figure out how much Allura means to me. When her parents passed away, they passed on to me a true gem. I've lived with Allura for five years now, and I tell you, she's special. Since I'm passing her on to you, I need you to promise me that Allura will be well taken care of. She's been through quite a lot in her life, as you're already aware, and I want her to be happy and secure from now onwards."

"Aunt Nahed, don't worry about Allura. She will be my love, my wife, my friend and my partner. Rest assured, I will take good care of her."

"I hope so, my son, because Allura is really precious," said Nahed, her voice overflowing with emotion.

"Oh, my dearest Nahed, I completely relate to what you're feeling right now. It's hard to see your baby grow up so fast," said Rasha.

Rasha was highly impressed with how organised and refined Nahed's house was. She had observed how disciplined her employees were and noticed that she had quite a few people working for her at the house, including the front door porter, who had greeted them upon their arrival to the mansion. She also picked up on Nahed's expensive taste and priceless antique collection. This laid to rest any concerns she had about Allura's prospects as a suitable bride for her only son.

"Ladies and gentlemen, lunch is served in the garden," announced the butler.

"Thank you, Osman. We'll be there shortly," Nahed said, dismissing him.

"Very well, madame," he replied before retreating.

Nahed stood up gracefully. "Well, shall we?"

The group made their way to the garden, exchanging light conversation before admiring the set-up that greeted them. The large table was practically groaning under the weight of the fine cutlery and dining set, while crystal flutes glittered in the sunlight.

"This is all so beautiful, Nahed," said Rasha as they took their seats.

"Thank you, Rasha. You're too kind," Nahed responded as servants bustled around, scooping the first course onto their plates.

Throughout the lunch, conversation flowed smoothly as the group flitted from topic to topic.

"So my dear, have you thought about what type of wedding you'd like to have?" Rasha asked curiously, turning to look at Allura.

"Oh, well, I'd rather have a small, intimate wedding, with family and a few close friends," replied Allura.

"But dear, part of our Egyptian tradition is for the bride and groom to be greeted by everyone at the *zaffa*. Nowadays, there are different types of *zaffas*, but it would be nice to have a traditional one, with a parade of belly dancers and drummers accompanying you to your *kosha* chairs, where you would appear like a king and queen surveying your kingdom – well, surveying your guests, at least," explained Rasha.

"That sounds very noisy and tiring, Aunt Rasha; plus, I'm not comfortable with everyone staring at me, and with all those video cameras focused on my face. It sounds like a lot of pressure to take on. I want to enjoy my wedding day, not worry about others' expectations."

"But that's our culture, Allura. What would people think?"

"Mother, please! Let Allura choose what she wants. Anyway, I agree with her. A large wedding is very stressful and a complete waste of money," interrupted Ahmed.

Allura shot him a grateful look. She didn't want to argue with her future mother-in-law already, but at the same time, there were some things she was just uncomfortable doing.

"I'm surprised you feel that way, Ahmed, given the importance of your father's position in the country. We need to invite very important delegates to this wedding. What do we tell them? 'Sorry, the bride and groom want to keep it simple; you're not invited'?" Rasha said sharply.

"Exactly, Mother. That's what we tell them if they ask. Besides, they have no right to ask. This is our special day, Allura's and mine. No one has the right to interfere or question what we choose to do. We are the only ones who are meant to be happy on that particular day. We are not doing this for the delegates. We are doing this for ourselves," said Ahmed.

"Come now, let's not ruin this pleasant lunch. We can discuss these details later," interjected Nahed.

"You're right; tell me more about this dessert. I've never seen such a pastry before," Shawki added awkwardly.

The conversation returned to blander topics until it was time for the Barakats to leave. Nahed and Allura accompanied them to the door, where Ahmed took the opportunity to apologise for his mother's discourtesy.

"It's quite all right, Ahmed. We understand. Weddings are usually grand affairs. God knows I've seen some doozies back in the day. But don't let any of us pressure you both into changing your plans and decisions, whether now or after you're married," Nahed said, glancing at their intertwined hands.

"Of course, Aunt Nahed. We will respect your opinions and do our best to compromise, but in the end, we'll do things the way we feel best suits us," said Ahmed. "Well, thank you again for agreeing to see us and accepting my proposal, and thank you for a delicious lunch. I'll speak to you soon, Allura."

"Good night, Ahmed," she said before shutting the door.

"Oh my God, Aunt Nahed, she seems very difficult!" Allura said, turning to her aunt anxiously.

"What mother-in-law isn't difficult, Allura? It's like that all over the world. There are obviously varying intensities, but generally there is no perfect mother-in-law."

"You think so? She seems very controlling. I don't know if I can handle that."

"Are you already having second thoughts, young lady?" Aunt Nahed chuckled. "Allura, dearest, this is just the beginning for you. As the Egyptian saying goes, when you marry a man, you marry into his family; you must make sure you deal with his mother in a respectful manner, regardless of what she does or says."

"I would never disrespect her. But I do have the right to voice my concerns or express my opinion, right?"

"Some words are better left unsaid, Allura, especially when it comes to dealing with older people. Just let things go. That is my advice to you if you want to get along with Ahmed's mother. I do agree, though, that she does not seem to be very easy to deal with."

"I guess. I just hope she doesn't try to interfere too much in our lives."

"Don't worry, Allura. I'm sure you'll find a way to keep her satisfied without compromising what you want."

"Thanks, Auntie. If you don't mind, I'm going to change into something more comfortable."

"That's a splendid idea. Come find me once you're done."

"Yes, Auntie Nahed."

Back in her bedroom, Allura bit her lip in apprehension as she mulled over the day's events while removing the heavy makeup that caked her face.

Toying with her mobile phone, she sent a quick e-mail to Bassel before she could change her mind:

***

Hey there cowboy,

So have you reached Texas yet? You said that you have a competition there. Hope all went well. Actually, I'm sure you came in first place; you always were a fierce competitor. You know, I just imagined you wearing a cowboy hat in just your swimming trunks. LOL.

Anyway, guess who just left our house? Ahmed and his parents. They were over to propose. All went well till his mother decided to butt in and suggest a zaffa and kosha for our wedding. She suggested a big wedding because they have a lot of important people they'd like to invite. When I disagreed with her, she became very angry. Ahmed stood up for me, which I liked very much. He was supportive and said, "Whatever Allura wants goes."

Speaking of which, I suggested a small wedding on a Nile cruise, inviting very close friends, and family, of course. You have to come, Bassel, please! We spoke about having a wedding in September, so that leaves you plenty of time to get things sorted before you travel.

Can't wait to hear all your news. Write back as soon as you can!

Love, A

***

Half an hour later, Bassel replied.

***

Hey girl!

How goes? So your big day is coming up soon. God, I can't believe you're getting married in three months! You make me feel old all of a sudden.

I am not sure I can make it to the wedding, to be honest. These upcoming months are the most critical for me, when I either make it or break it. But I'll try my best and will let you know.

Your MIL sounds awful. She sounds like trouble. I still think you're rushing things, but since you're sure about going ahead with it, here's my advice: Stick to your guns, do your thing and persist with your beliefs. To hell with her. I am glad Ahmed is man enough to stand up for you. If he doesn't stand up for you now, he never will.

I love the Nile cruise idea. And why do you have to invite anyone at all? Just go with him alone on the trip! Who needs company on a wedding night?

Take care,
Bassel

***

Chapter 21

The Honeymoon

It was finally the big day. Allura and Ahmed spent their wedding night on the Nile in a romantic cruise, with just Nahed, Shawki, and Rasha keeping them company, exactly the way Allura had envisioned. The next day, Allura and Ahmed flew to Paris for their honeymoon. The first four days were heavenly. Ahmed took Allura to the Louvre Museum, Eiffel Tower, Euro Disney and to a romantic boat cruise across the Seine River. They also watched the famous Moulin Rouge show.

Allura was ecstatic. She had always read about the city of romance and heard a lot about it from her mother. Paris was special for her in different ways. She quickly fell under its enchanting spell; it seemed that there was always something more magical around the corner. She couldn't believe how much Ahmed was spoiling her or the fact that she was now Mrs Allura Barakat.

On the sixth day of their trip, Ahmed had decided to take Allura on a morning helicopter tour to Versailles. Allura was extremely excited about the idea and looked forward to seeing all the famous French landmarks from up above, like the Seine River and Bois de Boulogne in addition to the Trocadero, Montparnasse, La Defense and the striking Eiffel Tower.

Much to her dismay, just as they were about to board the helicopter, Ahmed received a phone call from his father, who asked him to book the next flight back to Egypt. His mother had suffered from a stroke and was crying hysterically, demanding to see her son before something else happened to her.

As they rushed to the airport, Allura asked: "Ahmed, did Uncle Shawki say which hospital she's in? What happened, exactly?"

"I'm not sure, Allura. The second I heard she had a stroke, I hung up. My only concern now is to find a flight back to Egypt and see my mother."

Luckily, there was a flight due to depart in three hours. Ahmed and Allura spoke very little during the trip back to Egypt. Upon their arrival to the airport, they quickly went through customs using Ahmed's VIP connections before meeting the family driver outside.

As soon as the car pulled away, Ahmed called his father. "Dad, how's Mother?"

"She's fine. She had a minor stroke and spent two days in the hospital. We wanted to make sure everything was all right before sending her back home. She's at home resting now," Shawki replied.

"What happened exactly? What did the doctors say?"

"She had a transient ischaemic attack, which is a minor stroke. It only lasted a few minutes. We initially worried because she felt dizzy and the right-hand side of her face, arms, and legs started to feel numb. She was also finding it hard to speak, but she's on the mend now. The doctor anticipates she'll be fine."

"Great, thank God. Can we see her?"

"Of course you can see her. She's constantly asking about you. If only to shut her up for a bit, pass by the house and put her mind to ease."

"Yes, Father, we're on our way. We'll be there soon."

Allura searched her husband's face for a sign of what he was thinking.

"Ahmed? Honey? Is everything OK?"

"Of course it's not! My mother's just had a stroke!" Ahmed yelled, causing her to shrink back in fright.

Realising he had frightened her, Ahmed pinched his nose in an attempt to calm down. "I'm sorry, Allura. I'm just worried about her."

"It's OK, Ahmed. I completely understand your concern. Where is she now?"

"At home resting."

"So it's nothing serious?"

"Of course it's serious! A TIA could turn into a major stroke, especially if not monitored and treated promptly. I'm glad my mother expressed herself on the spot when she started to feel this way!"

Allura tried to quell her rising resentment against the ill woman. She didn't need to kick up such a fuss about seeing Ahmed after such a minor incident, especially since her husband was already taking care of her.

"If you'd prefer, you can meet her alone today and let her have some quality time with you. I can visit tomorrow and check up on her."

"Are you kidding? Do you forget that you're my wife now? Allura, grow up. Of course not. You need to be with me. Mother will be highly offended if I visit her without you."

Ahmed spoke in a sharp tone. Allura chose to believe that he was just on edge about the unfortunate news he had just received.

"OK, honey, I will not leave you. Of course, I'll tag along if you need me. I just didn't want to get in the way."

Rasha was lying in bed reading a magazine when Ahmed and Allura arrived. The second she saw Ahmed, she began to weep: "Oh my son, thank God you made it before anything were to happen to me." Ahmed approached his mother and kissed her hands, which he had done as a sign of respect since he was a little boy. She hugged him tight as she continued to let out tears.

"My son, thank you for coming. I missed you. Thank you, God, for bringing me back my son," said Rasha, raising her arms in supplication.

Allura lurked in the doorway, offering them some privacy. A part of her still resented how her mother-in-law had forced them to cut back on their lovely honeymoon, but another part was touched by how close the two suddenly seemed. The scene reminded Allura of her interactions with her own mother.

After a few minutes, Ahmed beckoned. "Allura, dear, get closer. Hug Mum."

"Hello, Aunt Rasha. I am sorry to hear about what happened to you. I wish you a speedy recovery," said Allura as she kissed Rasha on her cheeks.

"Thank you, my child. I am sorry to have disturbed your honeymoon. I really needed to see my son."

"I completely understand. Actually, it's good you disturbed it. Now, Ahmed owes me another honeymoon." Allura and Ahmed laughed, but Rasha didn't seem amused.

"It's not very nice to make fun out of my condition, especially since it seems I might get another stroke, and it could be a worse one. I could deteriorate completely."

"Oh, but I didn't mean to make fun out of you, Aunt Rasha. Sorry if it sounded that way."

"Mother, don't talk like that. You'll be just fine."

"It's true, Ahmed. And with your father always so busy at the centre, I'm left all alone to recover in this big house with no one to care for me."

"That's not true. You've got the nurses who visit and Father, and of course me and Allura. Remember? We live nearby, so we can always be here quickly if you need anything."

"I have another idea. This house is huge. We have five empty bedrooms. How about you stay with us for a while? I really need the company, and when you were off on your honeymoon, it felt very empty without you around."

"But Mother, I hardly spent time in this house before getting married to Allura. And it's not like we spent time together when I was growing up. Why should anything change now?"

Allura bit her tongue. She was angry that Rasha was trying to guilt Ahmed into moving into the family home, which, by all accounts, didn't hold many good memories for her new husband.

"Things have changed now, son, I'm sick!"

Ahmed pinched his nose. "Fine. But only for a few weeks or so. Is that all right, Allura? Mom wants to be pampered a bit."

Allura was disheartened by his response. It felt like he had already decided and was just asking her opinion out of courtesy. Before she could respond, Rasha exclaimed: "Oh, my precious ones, thank you! We already have a guest room set-up for the two of you. Just give me a minute. I'll ask the housemaid to take your stuff and move it in the room. You have no idea how happy you both made me just now."

"It's OK, Mother. Don't exert yourself. We'll take our luggage to the room ourselves. Which one is it?"

"It's the one at the end of the corridor. I chose the furthest room for you two; you obviously need your privacy."

Rasha had clearly arranged for this moment. She had already prepared the guest room and kept it clean and ready for Allura and Ahmed. She was not going to take 'no' for an answer and had planned accordingly.

"How thoughtful. Thank you, Aunt Rasha," responded Allura with a subtle smile. She meant to sound diplomatically sarcastic.

As soon as they entered the room, Allura shut the door behind them and turned to her husband angrily. "I cannot believe you, Ahmed! How could you agree to this situation? We're newlyweds, for crying out loud!"

"Why are you so worked up? I said that it was for just a couple of weeks! Anyway, if you didn't want to, you should've said something!"

"How could I say anything? Your mother's sick and in bed. That would have been very insensitive of me to do!"

"Exactly! If I leave my mother now when she needs me the most, that'll just show you that I can leave you someday when you need me the most."

Allura pursued her lips in frustration.

"Don't worry, darling. It is temporary, I promise you. Just relax and try to think positive. You're doing something good for an elderly woman. God will reward you. Would you like me to ask the driver to drop you to your aunt's house? I'm sure you miss her very much!"

"Yes, that would be nice. I'll go as soon as I'm done unpacking everything."

"All right, darling, I'll speak to him now," said Ahmed as he went to search for the driver.

Allura fought back tears as she began to unpack. This wasn't a positive start to their marriage, and she hoped that Ahmed would keep his promise to move them out soon. She couldn't help but think of how conniving her mother-in-law was. The thought of her made her body shiver.

Chapter 22

A Home Away from Home

Nahed was watering the flowers in the front patio when Allura approached her for a surprise visit.

"Allura? My darling Allura, it really is you! What a beautiful surprise! How are you? Let me look at you! Where's that honeymoon glow?" Nahed said with a tender look on her face.

"Oh, Aunt Nahed, I missed you. This is about the longest time away from you since I first moved in. It feels so good to be here again. This still feels like home to me, since I don't have a real home as yet."

"What do you mean, you don't have a home yet?" she asked while delicately removing her gardening gloves.

"Well, Ahmed's mum insisted we stay with her for a few days, so I haven't literally moved into my own house just yet."

"She did not! What on earth would she do that for? And why did you cut your honeymoon short? Let's go sit down. Come, dear," suggested Nahed as she escorted Allura to her preferred corner in the courtyard.

"She's not feeling well. She had a minor stroke which inconveniently interrupted our long-awaited honeymoon. Oh well, Ahmed promised that within a few weeks we'll move to our own house. Cross fingers!"

"I'm sorry to hear that. As awful as this sounds, her timing is dreadful, having a stroke on your honeymoon! Anyway, I'll phone her later to check up on her. How is she doing now?"

"She's fine, I guess. Ahmed isn't leaving her side. He's a great son."

Nahed examined the despondent woman before. If she didn't know better, she wouldn't have thought that Allura had just returned from her honeymoon.

"Of course it's good that he's a good son. But I don't want to talk about him, let's change the topic shall we? Now tell me all about Paris!"

"Paris is stunning. I kept remembering Mum's descriptions about how gorgeous the city is. I would have liked to see more of it, though. Speaking of which, I got you a little something from there. Hope you like it!"

Allura excitedly handed over a souvenir bag to her aunt. It was a Swarovski Eiffel Tower masterpiece, entirely designed in clear crystal, which she knew her aunt was fond of.

"Allura, you shouldn't have," commented Nahed. "Wow, this is beautiful. I haven't seen anything quite like it. Thank you, sweetheart."

An hour later, the house echoed with the women's laughter as Allura shared entertaining stories about her honeymoon over a bottle of red wine. Their conversation was interrupted, however, when Osman came in to tell Nahed that she had unexpected guests.

"Who are they, Osman? Did you not ask?"

"I did, madame. They said it was a surprise."

"Um, I'm not exactly dressed to impress, nor am I ready to accommodate anyone right now. Come along, Allura. Let's go see who these surprise guests might be. Get your glass with you as a form of self-defence just in case they turn out to be intruders," giggled Nahed.

The second Nahed spotted the guests she greeted them with sincerity. "Oh my Gosh, I cannot believe my eyes. Loula, my love, and Marwan! My darlings! Are you actually here in my home, after all those years?"

Loula and Marwan were Nahed's cousins, which made them part of Allura's family.

"Allura, meet Loula and Marwan. They are my ultimate favourite family members. And, God rest his soul, your father, adored them. They were at the funeral that day. Do you remember them?"

"Honestly, Auntie Nahed, I don't remember anyone from the funeral. I didn't look around much. I was too absorbed."

"Allura, my dear, you look wonderful! Wow, look at you. You've grown so much since I last saw you. Come here." Loula stepped forward and hugged Allura tightly.

The couple spent about an hour with Nahed and Allura, exchanging giggles and beautiful memories. Allura was ecstatic to have the chance to meet some of Haitham's relatives and remembered her mother's words about how important it was to be close to family.

"If Marwan and I had known that Allura was here, we would have definitely brought a special wedding gift with us. Allura, you must give me your new address. I promise to pay you a visit soon," said Loula.

"Why are you leaving so soon, my dearest? We didn't get enough of you. This visit doesn't count!" said Nahed.

"We were in the area, which is why we decided to pass by. You know we hardly come to Cairo. Honestly, we were unprepared. We didn't even expect to find you at home, but we said we'd try our luck and we indeed, got lucky," explained Marwan.

The couple lived in Alexandria, which was about two hours away from Cairo.

Allura made sure to exchange numbers with Aunt Loula. She was eager to meet the rest of the family and perhaps befriend them someday.

Nahed and Allura accompanied the family members all the way to the front gate, till they got into their car and drove away.

"It feels so good to meet some of the family, Auntie Nahed. It almost makes me feel like Mum and Dad are around again. We need to make more effort into going to Alexandria or wherever it is to visit all our family members."

"You're right, Allura. I was wrong not to encourage that earlier. Now, let's go back and indulge in our interrupted conversation."

Just then, Allura's phone rang. It was Ahmed, requesting her to return back home.

"Oh, Allura, chin up. I know things may seem tough now, but remember: it's a temporary situation. You know you could always come back here if you ever needed to get away," suggested Nahed as they shared a bittersweet hug.

"Thank you, Auntie. You've always been a ray of sunlight in my life."

"Oh, dear child, you're a part of my heart and soul, Allura. Never forget that."

"Aunt Nahed, can I ask to see my bedroom before leaving?"

"Are you even asking? Allura, this is your home. It always has been and always will be."

Allura rushed up to her room excitedly to find everything in its place, just the way she had left it. She loved her room, the house and her aunt. It felt safe to get reacquainted with what once belonged to her.

As the Barakats' town car drove away, Allura looked back wistfully at her previous home. Already it seemed that things were never going to be the same again.

Walking into her in-laws' house, Allura found Ahmed lying on the living room couch absorbed in some work he was finishing off on his laptop.

"Hi, honey," said Allura with a smile as she approached him for a kiss.

Ahmed's nose crinkled. "Allura, have you been drinking?"

"Yes, why?"

"I don't like that, Allura. The second you're left alone or go to your aunt's house, you end up drinking. You're a loose cannon!"

"Excuse me? You know I have the occasional drink. How is it different now?"

"Well, not anymore, and not while you're my wife. I want God to bless our marriage and home. You seem to forget that it's a huge sin to drink alcohol in our religion. No more drinking, Allura, please."

"I'm surprised, Ahmed. You've always known that I drink occasionally, from the moment you met me. Why the sudden orders and attitude?"

"It's not sudden. I never liked the fact that you drink. Maybe I never expressed that to you openly, but I just don't think it's right to drink. And since you are my wife now, it is my right to tell you what I dislike from here on."

"It is not your right to tell me what to do and what not to do, or how to live my life, especially since you never told me before that this bothered you. It's like you're two different people all of a sudden: the tolerant, patient, understanding man before we got married, and this conservative, snappy, demanding person the second there's a ring on my finger!"

Ahmed shrugged. "I cannot believe that you're actually arguing with me over alcohol. Does it mean that much to you to have a bloody drink? What are you, an alcoholic? Allura, I'm reading something important right now. If you don't mind, I'd like some privacy. No more arguments about this: No more drinking, and that's the end of this conversation."

Allura was incensed. Where had the sweet, open-minded man she had always confided in gone? So what if she had a few drinks with her aunt? Ahmed knew she had the occasional glass of wine or spirits. Why did it suddenly bother him so much that he practically commanded her to stop? Taking a deep breath, Allura counted to ten. It had been a stressful couple of days; hopefully, things would get better tomorrow. And if they didn't, then she'd deal with everything one day at a time.

Chapter 23

It Takes Courage to Pursue a Dream

As luck would have it, Rasha's health improved tremendously over the next couple of weeks, which meant that the newlyweds could finally move into their own home.

Allura was relieved to move out of Rasha and Shawki's rather depressing house, where she felt imprisoned. Her mother-in-law got under her skin. Everything about her made Allura uncomfortable. It was stressful trying to put on an act and remain courteous.

She could finally start her life properly as a married woman and let Ahmed deal with the petty things like checking up on Rasha. But even being the queen of her domain came with a new set of challenges. For one, even though Ahmed employed a maid and cook, Allura still preferred to cook and clean herself, which was bewildering to the house staff. That routine became rather boring quickly, though, and Allura found herself fantasising about a life outside the house.

"Honey, I feel it's time to start looking for a job. I'm getting bored with staying home like this. Plus, I need to make use of that degree I've just earned," said Allura tentatively, conscious of the fact that Ahmed's favourite football team was currently defending their title on the screen.

"Bored? Already? I thought we had agreed that you'd take time off to unwind. Besides, why do you need to work? I make enough money to sustain the two of us for a lifetime."

"It's not about money, Ahmed. It's about me. I need to keep myself occupied and improve my qualifications. I didn't study for practically half my life to throw my education away like that."

"Keep yourself busy at home or go to the social club and meet your friends."

"I don't understand why you are against me working. What's the big deal with me working?"

"I am doing this for your sake. Any woman would love to be in your place and do nothing but spoil herself. Work has become stressful these days, and people have become aggressive. I don't want your beautiful and innocent nature to disappear, nor do I want you nervous around the house."

"That's ridiculous, Ahmed. I've never heard anything so absurd! Let me pursue my master's degree, at the least!"

"Absurd? Allura, speak to me with some respect. Don't forget, I am your husband, and you need to watch your words around me. I will think about the master's degree. Give me some time to weigh it in my mind."

"But Ahmed—"

"I said enough, Allura! Let me watch the game in peace. You just made me miss an important part!" he huffed.

Allura jumped in surprise. It seemed as though Ahmed was changing more and more each day, and she didn't know what to make of his personality shift. It might be due to his mum's stroke or stress from work. He'll calm down, she reasoned. In the meantime, she'd find other ways to distract herself.

Over the next few days, Allura tried to fill her time up by doing some research for her master's degree. She was also busy reading, cooking and cleaning the house, trying to find anything to prevent her from interacting with Ahmed. One day, he returned home in a jubilant mood.

"Honey, I've got great news!"

"What is it?"

"I was offered a partnership in the centre, which I was given permission to expand further. It's a dream I've had since I was a child, to expand the family business."

"That's lovely news, hon! I am very happy for you."

"I could've never done it without your support."

"My support?"

"Yes, all those years when you've listened to me and advised me, and especially now as my wife."

"I was simply listening to you as you spoke, which is a natural thing to do. God only knows, you've had your own share of listening to me whine away throughout the past few years. I appreciate you feeling that way, and I am so proud to hear it. Thank you, babe."

"No, thank you! So how about we celebrate tonight? Honestly, I would give you the stars and the moon just about now!"

Allura found it an opportunity to remind her husband about her situation. "How about giving me a chance to study?"

His good mood vanished abruptly.

"Again, Allura? Don't you get bored of nagging?"

"You said you'd think about me studying for my master's degree. I'd still like to apply for the programme. There's still a couple of weeks left till deadline."

"No, Allura. Not this semester. I already hardly see you. You're always cooking or cleaning, or doing something in some corner of the house other than spending time with me. If you start studying too, it'll be like I'm a widower – but my wife's still alive!"

"That's not fair. I'm doing my best to be a good wife for you. Why won't you give this to me?"

"Well, how about this, then? Come and work at the centre with me. That way you'll be working, and we'll get to spend time together. Not to mention, you'll let the staff actually do their jobs."

"That's a sweet offer, and I'd love to spend more time with you. It's just…I'd like to focus on my own career more, instead of just being someone who just follows you wherever you go. Speaking of which, I've already received an offer alongside studying for my master's degree."

Ahmed's eyebrows rose in surprise. "Oh? As what? Where?"

"Assistant to the head of the university's journalism and mass communications department."

"Really now? When were you going to tell me you had even applied for that position? It's not nice to keep secrets in a marriage, Allura."

"I didn't apply. They approached me when I was inquiring about my master's degree in journalism and mass communications a few days ago. I never took it seriously. I even forgot about it. Today I checked my e-mail and found an official offer. To be honest, I feel blessed. It's a great chance to study and work in the same place."

Ahmed stood silently.

"Well? Can I accept, Ahmed?"

He pursed his lips before nodding his acceptance. "I'm only going to agree just to get you to stop nagging this way. My God, Allura, when you really want something, you don't stop. You don't give up easy, do you?"

Allura giggled.

"You're right about that one. Thank you, Ahmed. I promise I won't let it interfere with my duties as your wife!"

"You're welcome, Allura. Just don't make me regret this, OK?"

"I won't!" Allura kissed him gleefully before bounding to the laptop to send off her acceptance.

Allura was exactly where she wanted to be, studying and working in her first real job. She would be reporting to Professor Jennings, a distinguished fellow who had over thirty years' experience in media relations and writing. The job would offer a wealth of knowledge for her to learn from.

Her life was almost complete, and her dreams were actually becoming a reality.

Days later, during one of her classroom breaks, Allura decided to check up on Bassel on WhatsApp. She hadn't heard from him in quite some time.

'Hey there stranger, where have you been? How's life treating you? I hope you're doing all right.'

Bassel responded immediately.

'Hey, soul sista! What up? I wanted to text you a couple of times but wasn't sure when would be best. Plus, now that you're married and all, I wasn't sure if it was even appropriate anymore.'

'Are you kidding? Of course you can message me. We're friends! Plus, Ahmed knows you, so it isn't a problem. At least I hope it isn't.'

'Oh? Trouble in paradise already, Mrs Barakat?'

'Kinda, I guess.'

'Why, what's the matter? I'm sorry to hear that, Allura. I really am.'

'Marriage isn't quite what I expected, I guess. Bassel, you might be right. I might not be cut out to be a wife.'

'What ever happened to your swarming emotions? Listen, Allura, you've only been married for a few months now. Give yourself some slack! What does the problem seem to be, anyway?'

'It feels like Ahmed's extremely selfish and controlling. He just wants me all to himself. He was against me working and pursuing my master's degree because he was afraid it would affect my duties as a housewife. Like, please! Who thinks that way these days?'

'Hmmmm, I didn't peg him to be such a conservative person. What happened?'

'I don't know. I mean, he had a weird childhood growing up, like he was neglected or something. But it seems like he kept this side of his personality hidden until it was too late. It's like I married Dr Jekyll and Mr Hyde.'

'You never noticed any signs of his current attitude earlier? I find that hard to believe. You've known him for quite a bit now.'

'No, I didn't. On the contrary, he was extremely polite, gentle, and…what can I say? He was a dream come true. He was perfect! I really don't know what to make out of it. It's just weird!'

Suddenly, Allura felt a rush of nausea. She hurried to the bathroom and barely made it to the toilet bowl, holding onto it for what felt like an eternity.

After it seemed her stomach didn't have anything more to throw up, Allura freshened up before excusing herself to

Professor Jennings and heading home. Her previous conversation with Bassel had slipped her mind completely as she thought about what could've caused such a strong reaction. Concerned, she decided to phone Nahed.

"Hello, Allura. What a pleasant surprise. How are you doing today?"

"Auntie Nahed. Are you free right now?"

"Is something wrong? You don't sound yourself."

"I'm not sure. I suddenly feel very sick. It could be something I ate for lunch. I'm on my way to the clinic. Can you please meet me there? I don't want to disturb Ahmed. He's very busy nowadays."

"Of course, I'll be there. But once we're sure everything's OK, I think you should tell Ahmed that you're not feeling well."

"It's probably nothing, and he's – well, chances are, he's busy in ongoing meetings." Before Allura could continue her argument, she let out a pained groan.

"Allura? Allura?"

"Uh, yes. I'm here, Auntie. Please try to make it there fast."

"When you get to the clinic, stay in the waiting room. I want to be there when you speak to the doctor."

"I think it may be food poisoning. I'm bloated and feel sick to the stomach."

"I'll dress and meet you there, Allura. It won't take me long. See you soon."

"Thanks, Auntie Nahed, see you."

As soon as she arrived, Allura was given a cup of water to sip on as she filled out some routine paperwork.

"Allura? Allura? Where are you?"

"I'm here, Auntie, literally in front of you."

"Oh, there you are. You gave me quite a scare! How are you feeling now, dear? What happened?"

Allura began describing how she felt, stopping when she noticed her aunt's pale expression.

"Auntie Nahed? Are you OK?"

"Allura, I'm going to ask you something. It's rather sensitive, but I need you to answer honestly."

"Um."

"Have you and Ahmed been using protection?"

"Auntie!"

"Just answer the question!"

"No, I didn't really think of it!"

Nahed laughed. "What do you mean, you didn't think of it! Honey, I think you may just be pregnant."

"Pregnant?" Allura was in shock. She had never even thought about the idea. "You think so?"

Just then, Allura heard the nurse call her name out.

"Come on, sweetie. Let's see what the doctor says," said Nahed as she guided the dazed woman.

Several tests later, the gynaecologist confirmed Nahed's suspicions; Allura was eight weeks pregnant.

"Congratulations, honey, you're going to be a mother! And at last, I'm going to be a grandmother!" Nahed said joyfully.

"How did this happen?" Allura and Ahmed had been taking the intimacy lane pretty slow. Given her previous experience, which had left her daunted, she didn't feel very comfortable rushing into things.

"What do you mean, how did this happen? You're a married lady now, Allura."

"I know, Auntie Nahed, but I don't understand how it could have happened this fast. We only just got married and have hardly spent any intimate time together."

"It only takes one time for this to happen. Besides, don't think of the how; just enjoy the now. You are about to be a mum, which is the most amazing gift a woman could ever wish for. Enjoy it, darling, and think of how you'll break the news to your husband."

A million thoughts crossed Allura's mind. She had always said that she couldn't wait to start a family, but now that she was pregnant, she had her doubts. She had just begun her career and life as a married woman, and now she was going to be saddled with a baby.

Allura arrived home confused but determined to break the happy news to Ahmed. First, she had to make sure he was in a good mood. So she cooked his favourite meal, the famous Egyptian dish *molokhia*, and dressed up before waiting for him to come through the door.

Upon walking into the house, Ahmed noticed the change in atmosphere. As he placed a soft kiss on her forehead, he said: "Wow, what smells so good? And you look amazing!"

Gazing at the lit candles neatly placed on the dinner table, Ahmed grew apprehensive. "Uh oh, is there some sort of anniversary I've forgotten about?"

"I just felt like preparing a special meal for you today. I'm in one of those exceptionally happy moods."

"Wow, nice. Thank you, love. How I wish you would be this happy each and every single day of our lives." Ahmed grinned as he reached out to embrace his wife. "But honey, I've got to get back to the centre. I have an important appointment in an hour at the clinic."

"What? You just got here! I even prepared your favourite meal!"

"I'm sorry, sweetie. I can eat it when I get back. I came back home to pick up a few papers. I'm studying a complicated case of Parkinson's disease, and now that I'm on the board of directors, there's a lot more pressure on me. I was just passing by to pick up some research papers that I wanted to discuss at the meeting this evening."

"Tonight? This can't wait till tomorrow? I miss you, Ahmed!"

"I know. I miss you too. I'm very sorry, Allura. I'll try to be back as soon as I can."

"How long will it take?"

"I don't think it should take more than two to three hours."

Allura watched in disappointment as Ahmed rushed out of the house, haphazardly clutching several papers. She had wanted to set the mood just right before breaking the news to him, but now it seemed that she would just have to wait.

Chapter 24

Darkness and Light

The next day, Ahmed woke Allura up with a tender kiss. "Honey, I am so sorry about last night. You know how busy work is these days. I hope you're not too mad at me."

Allura rubbed her eyes and yawned before coming to her senses. "Yes, I am mad at you. I had something very special to share with you yesterday, and you completely bailed out on me."

"Really? What is it? I'm sorry. Let me make it up to you."

"No, I'm not in the mood right now."

"Don't be like that. How about I fix you a cup of coffee and you tell me your big news? I even promise to turn my phone off, and perhaps…give you a massage?"

"Umm, coffee sounds good, but I'll skip on the massage."

"Fair enough, I'll be right back."

Ahmed rushed to prepare her favourite morning beverage. When he returned, though, the smell of caffeine turned Allura's stomach, and she stumbled into the bathroom.

"Let it out, sweetie. That's it. Oh, Allura, are you feeling a bit better? I had no idea my morning coffee would make you this sick," Ahmed said as he soothed her wracking body.

"Well, that's not exactly how I wanted you to find out," she said after calming down.

"Find out what?" Ahmed paused for a few seconds. "No! You're joking! Are you—"

"Pregnant! Yes, I'm pregnant, which is exactly why I wanted last night to be super special."

"Oh, honey!" Ahmed was over the moon. He couldn't believe what he had just heard. He'd always wanted to be a father. He carefully clutched Allura tightly to his chest and showered her with soft kisses.

"Thank you for bringing joy and happiness into my life. Thank you for all you've done and continue to do. This is about the best news I've heard. Just wait till I tell my parents about this."

Ahmed mistook her pained expression as something related to her morning sickness.

"Come on, let's get you back to bed. You need to rest as much as possible from now onwards, and we need to get you to a good doctor."

"I've already got a doctor I'm comfortable with. She works at the clinic that Auntie Nahed and I go to, and I'd like to keep seeing her. She already knows my history and everything."

"How come you didn't tell me about that doctor before?"

"I didn't think it was relevant to tell you about our family doctor! Besides, when I decided to pay them a visit I had no idea I was pregnant. I thought it was food poisoning or something, and I didn't want to disturb you in case it was something minor."

"You could never disturb me. From now on, whatever it is, you call me. Even if I can't be there with you, at least let me know what's going on."

"OK, I promise. But in this particular incident, well, I just wanted to surprise you," she said with a sincere smile.

"So that's why you wanted me to stay for dinner," he said thoughtfully.

"Yeah. Anyway, it's done. Now you know. Excuse me, I've got to eat something and take my folic acid pills."

"Stay right there. I'll get you some toast and camomile tea to settle your stomach, and I'll bring the pills. Today, I'm at your service. Whatever you need, just tell me."

Allura giggled. "That's a first. I quite like the sound of that," she teased.

Ahmed smiled. "Why, you wild beauty, you. Come here." He drew her closer to him, and they hugged each other fondly, revelling in the moment.

Allura moved her head backwards, allowing enough space for eye contact. "You've got to promise me that when our child's born, you'll cut back on your hours at the centre a little. I want it to know its father."

Allura knew of a lot of mums around her who had been forced to raise their children without the help of a father. "I find it extremely discriminatory when a woman has to handle it all by herself while her husband comes up with illogical excuses to refrain from taking care of his children."

"Of course, honey, anything you say. You just take good care of yourself for now, take your vitamins, and keep yourself happy and calm. We want a cute little healthy baby who looks just like its gorgeous mummy."

Days passed, and Allura became accustomed to life as a pregnant woman, which included repeated trips to the bathroom, no matter where she was. Thankfully, her peers and Professor Jennings were gracious about her condition.

In the meantime, Ahmed continued to work long hours at the office, which Allura resented greatly. It felt as though he was abandoning her and the baby already.

Things finally came to a head when Ahmed called one day to inform her that his parents were coming to congratulate them on their happy news.

"Darling, Mum and Dad would like to come over to congratulate us on the baby. From now on, can you please ask the cook to prepare things? Don't tire yourself."

"You know I like to cook myself when it comes to you or your guests, so imagine my own in-laws. I will cook. I have no issues with that. Do you mind if I ask my aunt to tag along?"

When she was younger, Allura had enjoyed hanging around the kitchen watching her mother cook both Egyptian and Lebanese food. The smell of food intrigued her, and she wanted to learn how to do it herself. Once she moved into Nahed's home, she would occasionally hang out in the kitchen and watch the chef at work. After marriage, it only took a few experiments before she started to master some of the major Egyptian dishes that Ahmed favoured the most.

"Of course I don't mind. The more the merrier," replied Ahmed.

"So what time should I expect them? Will you be able to be here on time, or will you catch up with us?"

"They should be here around six. I'll try to be here on time. I'll even try to leave work early if I can."

"All right. See you tonight."

Allura and her cook spent the day preparing various Egyptian and Lebanese dishes, including stuffed vine leaves served with a separate plate of yoghurt with cucumber and garlic on the side, eggplant, mixed rice with cashews, blue cheese stuffed chicken breast and different plates of salads, including the famous Lebanese salad *tabbouleh*, alongside assorted side dishes and dressings.

That evening, Allura greeted Rasha, Shawki and Nahed upon their arrival, explaining that Ahmed was running late and that he would catch up with them soon.

"I am very sorry about Ahmed not being here yet. I think that we should give it one more hour. If he's still not here by then, we should all begin to have dinner. Otherwise, the food will get cold," said Allura courteously to her three guests.

"Is Ahmed spending too much time at work lately?" asked Shawki.

"Yes, he's very busy these days. I guess expanding the business means more projects and patients," answered Allura diplomatically.

"That's right, we are pretty busy. It's an exciting time for us. But I hope that doesn't mean he spends less quality time with you?" inquired Shawki.

"You do know that Ahmed is working this hard in order to meet your and your baby's needs. It's only natural for him to be this ambitious in the beginning of your marriage. You shouldn't let something like this get between you. On the contrary, you should admire his eagerness to further raise your standard of living," Rasha added.

Allura nodded demurely, trying her best not to roll her eyes or act in an inappropriate manner towards her mother-in-law. Her spirits lifted slightly when Nahed gave her a subtle wink and shake of the head.

The hour passed, and Ahmed hadn't arrived yet, so Allura ushered everyone to the dining room. While they were eating, Ahmed called.

"Allura, I am so sorry I'm late. I had a last-minute meeting that I couldn't delay. I'm on my way home."

"That's fine, Ahmed. Take your time. We're already eating dinner. Drive home safely."

"Poor Ahmed, he's probably starving by now," commented Rasha as Allura hung up the phone.

Allura could feel her teeth grinding to a pulp. She was growing more annoyed with her mother-in-law with each passing day.

"He does work such long hours, but I make sure that there's something for him to eat when he gets home," she said pointedly.

"That's nice, dear. It's good you're taking your wifely duties seriously," Rasha responded dismissively.

Allura took a deep breath. While it would give her absolute pleasure to throw the plate of yoghurt at Rasha's face, she couldn't possibly insult her mother-in-law like that.

While they were eating dessert, Ahmed walked in.

"Good evening, everybody. I'm awfully sorry I'm late," he said as he kissed Allura's forehead.

"That's fine, dear. You're just working hard to make sure your wife and child are supported financially. Come, eat. I'm sure there's some leftover food for you," said Rasha as she attempted to fill an empty plate for Ahmed.

"Please, sit, Aunt Rasha. I insist. You're my guest; I'll have a quick word with the cook and reheat the food for Ahmed."

Allura rushed out, grateful for the excuse to get away from the room's heavy atmosphere. Returning, she placed a full plate of food in front of her husband before cleaning up the dirty dishes. Various conversations were filling the room.

Ahmed and Shawki were speaking about work, while Rasha spoke to Nahed about the latest cosmetic surgery trends. Despite both conversations being extremely boring for Allura, she kept her cool and remained gracious throughout the night.

Turning to look at her, Rasha commented: "Allura, dear, I noticed you haven't sat down all night. Did you forget that you're pregnant?"

"Thanks for your concern, Aunt Rasha. I feel that moving around is good for me, especially after meals. It makes me feel lighter."

"Not during your first trimester. The first few months of pregnancy are sensitive; you need to be very careful not to strain yourself too much."

"She's right, darling. Why don't you sit down? The cleaners will take care of everything. Why are you doing all of this yourself?" asked Ahmed.

"You know I like doing things myself, especially when it comes to the house. My being pregnant shouldn't change that. I'm not ill, Ahmed. I'm only pregnant."

Rasha barged in: "We understand that, but you haven't said even one word to us all evening because you're too busy with the housework!"

Things started to get strained at that point, and Allura was close to losing her temper until Nahed jumped in: "You know Allura…she's Miss Energiser Bunny. She can't sit still in one place, and if she did, she'd literally fall sick."

"That's when she wasn't pregnant, but now she needs to rest. She can't afford to run around like that," insisted Rasha.

Rasha just wouldn't stop, and Nahed was certain that Allura would lose her temper right there. Her heart dropped for a split second when Allura shuddered as she started to speak up. She prayed Allura would remain respectful in her response.

"With all due respect, Aunt Rasha, I feel just fine. I know what's best for my body, and I care more than anyone else in this room about the baby I'm carrying. The moment I feel like my body is aching or that I need to sit or rest, or whatever it is you are insisting I do, I'll do it. Till then, I'd appreciate it if everyone around me can be more supportive. As for not speaking with you all evening, I did speak with you while we were seated at the dinner table. Now that you and my aunt are speaking about plastic surgery, I find I don't have much to contribute."

Allura's tone was calm yet icy. It was obvious that Rasha had gotten under her skin. Ahmed and Shawki blamed it on her hormones. Nahed understood her feelings but chose to keep quiet. At that point, there was really nothing she could say or do.

There was a sudden stillness in the room for a few seconds till Rasha got up hastily, and without a single word, headed towards the door with tears in her eyes. Shawki and Ahmed stood up in alarm and rushed out to comfort the weeping woman.

"Mum, wait, wait. Don't leave like this!" pleaded Ahmed as he ran behind her.

"I am leaving like this!" she said while walking out of the door, sniffing. "Haven't you heard the way your beloved wife spoke to me in front of everyone just now? She's a child. How dare she speak to me in that tone? Is that what I deserve from you and your wife? This is the first time I have actually stepped foot into your new home – and possibly the last, after tonight."

"Come on, Mum, you're exaggerating. She was just trying to express herself. She didn't mean to disrespect you in any way. Don't ruin a good night, don't be overly sensitive."

Despite Ahmed's attempt to convince his mother to come back into the house to discuss things, Rasha insisted on leaving.

The second they all walked out of the door, Nahed turned to speak to Allura. "Didn't I tell you not to lose your temper and keep your cool with his mother? What's wrong with you? No matter what she does to annoy you, she's still older than you; you need to talk to her with respect. Plus, she's your husband's mother, and that doesn't look like it's about to change anytime soon. So what were you thinking, talking back to her that way?"

"I can't believe you're defending that double-faced witch after all the bitching around she's been pulling on me all night in front of you. And please don't tell me you didn't notice. Weren't you present tonight? Didn't you see her attitude and constant bickering? She's annoying, Aunt Nahed, and she's also controlling. She has no right to tell me what to do and what not to do with my body, especially in my own home!"

"Allura, you didn't sit still all night. You were highly strung in their presence and tried to avoid them altogether. Don't you think they felt that?"

"What do you want me to do? Her voice, her face, everything about her just irritates me. I wasn't brought up to challenge someone older than me, so instead I tried to avoid her. I did the best I could to be courteous during dinner, but when she started to speak about all those plastic surgery things I got so annoyed! We're here to celebrate the baby. She has to turn things to her and speak about herself all the time!"

"You are in no position to judge a woman old enough to be your mother – or even grandmother, for that matter. Allura, she's old. I told you before that you need to be diplomatic, especially around a woman like Rasha."

"Aunt Nahed, she's self-centred! Do you honestly think I'm the one who invited her here in the first place? She's the one who invited herself – and on short notice, too! If she really cared about my unborn child, as she claims, she wouldn't have insisted on visiting us for dinner today, acknowledging how tired I would naturally be during my first trimester. If she had any sense, she should have invited us to her house or to dine out. But no, she has to decide on short notice to annoy her son's pregnant wife! She just infuriates me. I can't stand her! And it's sad, because I don't have a mother. My mum is dead. Anyone else in her shoes would have tried to treat me like her own daughter. I really don't think I'm asking for much! I'm not a bad person, Aunt Nahed. I don't deserve this sort of bitterness from anyone."

"Allura, you chose to marry this man, and you know how it is here in Egypt. When you marry someone, you marry into his family, meaning you need to get along with them. You need to control yourself with his mother, regardless of what sort of woman she is. Now please, calm yourself down, and let's pray Ahmed manages to convince her to come back. Otherwise, things will spiral out of proportion unnecessarily."

"I am not in the wrong here, and I didn't disrespect her in any way. I was just asking her indirectly and in a polite manner to bug the hell off. She's been on my case all night. Aunt Nahed, are you on her side or mine? You were with us in the same room. Be fair!"

"On yours, silly girl. That's exactly why I need you to calm down and take a deep breath. I think your hormones are all worked up now. That's what happens during pregnancy." Nahed laughed as she softly touched Allura's hands. "Sweetheart, just relax, will you? Exhale, inhale. Take a deep breath in and out. Trust me, it'll make you feel better."

As Allura took a few breaths, Nahed prayed deep down inside that things would just pass. She felt sorry for Allura and knew that she was right. She had similar observations about Rasha but wanted to stay controlled and wise for Allura's sake. Her main mission for now was to calm Allura down so that she and Ahmed would remain happy.

Ahmed returned shortly without his parents.

"What did you do, Allura?" he yelled as his face twisted grotesquely.

Nahed stood in front of Allura protectively.

"Ahmed, please don't speak to your pregnant wife like that! Allura went out of her way to prepare a lovely meal for everyone today. I don't want to be a part of this argument, but if you don't calm down, we're going to have a problem," she said forcefully.

"Didn't you see how she spoke to my mother?"

"I did, Ahmed, and I just spoke to her about it. She didn't mean it to come out that way. She's just very tired and pregnant. This is all very new to her. Ahmed, please stay composed. I repeat, she's pregnant, and yelling is not in any way good for her or the baby."

"I don't care what her status is right now. How dare she speak to my mum that way?" He turned to Allura and said loudly, "Allura! How could you disrespect Mother that way?"

"I did nothing wrong, Ahmed! She was on my case from way before you arrived, and I was taking crap from her all night long. Eventually it just got to be too much. Sorry to say this, Ahmed, but your mother is a control freak. She wants to control everything and everyone around her, and I just can't take that kind of attitude anymore!"

"Now she left upset and probably won't come back to our house in a long time. Are you happy that way?"

"Don't turn this around. Your mum is not exactly a saint. She was rude too!"

Ahmed's face turned red, which made Nahed even more apprehensive.

"Allura, stop it now. Don't answer him back. Ahmed is obviously upset right now, and so are you. Just step away from the issue. Anything either of you say right now will turn out wrong."

Allura emerged from behind her aunt and began walking to Ahmed challengingly.

"No, Aunt Nahed. I am sick of him and his provocative mother taking sides against me all the time. I have been nothing but graceful and considerate to your mum, yet she's constantly bullying me."

"Respect yourself, Allura, and don't you dare speak or utter a word about my mother again! Do you hear me?" he rumbled.

At that point, Nahed grabbed Allura and pulled her back, terrified that Ahmed might be provoked to violence.

"Please, stop it. Both of you are getting loud and unreasonable. Nothing serious happened to warrant all this arguing. Just sleep on it, and I will speak to Rasha tomorrow morning and sort out everything. Allura, please, this is not like you. Just stop arguing. And Ahmed, if you don't mind, please stop raising your voice, especially in my presence. Don't forget that I'm an elderly woman. Kindly respect that," requested Nahed.

"I will speak to my wife in whatever way I want, and you will not interfere," Ahmed said, pushing Nahed aside and grabbing Allura's arm.

"Stop it! You're hurting me!" Allura scratched his arm, trying to break free.

"Shut your trap now! You spoilt, rude brat, you have no idea how to behave. But of course, how could you? No one was around long enough to bring you up properly!"

Ahmed unintentionally shoved Allura into a wall, causing her to bang her head and fall on her stomach.

The room grew silent for a split second, followed by Allura's pain-filled screams.

"Ah! My baby! I think I lost my baby!"

"Oh my God! Call an ambulance, now!" bellowed Nahed as Ahmed stood there in complete shock.

"There's no time!" Ahmed scooped up Allura and rushed her to the car with Nahed trailing behind.

Ahmed drove Allura and Nahed to an emergency care unit at a nearby hospital. Allura was already bleeding. Nahed kept praying aloud as she caressed her distraught great-niece, trying to reassure her.

Once they arrived, doctors performed a quick series of tests and examinations before confirming that Allura had lost the baby. Allura was told that she had to stay in the hospital for a few days for monitoring, to make sure she regained her strength. Her blood pressure was low, and she needed strong painkillers for the pain.

Nahed decided to stay with Allura at the hospital in a bed close to hers. Allura was very quiet. Tears rolled down her cheeks, and she hardly said a word. Ahmed had been banished from her sight. Allura didn't think she could even handle the mention of his name for the time being. However, despite her best attempts, she couldn't ignore the heated conversation outside her room.

"Ahmed, stay out of her sight for a while. When and if things calm down, I'll contact you. For now, you've done enough damage," said Aunt Nahed.

"Come on, that's not fair! This is just as hard on me, you know. Do you think I meant to push her towards the wall and lose my own baby? She lost her balance and ended up on the floor!"

"I am certain you didn't mean it, but this is how most abusive relationships start. And believe me, I will never allow you anywhere near my precious girl again until you find a way to control that temper of yours. She will stay with me until everything is resolved, and the only way I'll let her go back to you is if you first guarantee that something like this will never happen again. That's if she chooses to return to you."

"Who do you think you are to interfere in our marriage? Yes, I was wrong tonight. Believe me, I blame myself for everything. But I'm not some kind of monster! Things had been strained between us for a while, and everything just boiled over."

"I don't care about that. All relationships have their ups and downs. But the fact that you raised your hand to her, and in my presence, makes me feel like I can't trust you. Not anymore."

"Aunt Nahed! What more do you want me to say? I'm sorry. I hate myself for what happened. If I could turn back time I would! Tell me what I can do to make things right again!"

There was a pause.

"You can start by apologising to your wife and asking her and God's forgiveness for what happened. Then, you will leave her alone to heal, no matter how long that takes. Once, and only once, she's ready and willing to speak to you, can any contact be initiated between the two of you."

"Whatever you want, Aunt Nahed," said Ahmed in disappointment.

They returned to the room to find Allura facing away from them.

"Allura? Sweetheart? Can you please look at me for a moment?"

She sighed.

"OK, I know you're angry and upset and probably on meds, but I just want to say this before I go: I'm sorry. I'm so sorry. I was really looking forward to being a dad, and now I've ruined everything. I'll never forgive myself, but I hope you'll find it in your heart to forgive me. I love you, darling, and please believe me when I say that I really didn't mean to push you like that, it was the result of uncontrolled anger and bottled-up frustration, which I admit is unjustifiable." After a few seconds of no response, Ahmed said: "Fine, I understand your silence, and respect it, I'll leave you alone now, Allura."

At the sound of Ahmed's retreating, heavy footsteps, Allura began to sob heavily.

"Oh, oh, oh, my dear, sweet Allura. Come now, let it all out. Auntie Nahed's here, and everything's going to be all right again." Nahed rubbed Allura's arm soothingly.

Allura whiled away the rest of her hospital stay by filling up her journal. She wrote down her thoughts about losing her precious baby and memories of Ahmed's courtship of her and their marriage. Allura tried desperately to look for clues that she might have missed in all their years together.

She remembered the very first day she met him at the centre. She recalled how rude and proud he was until he looked up and found a pretty girl in front of him. She questioned his actions and his weak character in front of his mother. Above all, she questioned his reactions whenever things got a little stressful.

Nahed stayed in Allura's room but kept her distance, which Allura was grateful for. After everything that had happened, the younger woman needed some time alone.

After a few days, Allura was discharged from the hospital and returned to her aunt's house to recuperate further. Throughout this time, Ahmed had been regularly contacting Nahed about Allura's condition, which Nahed dutifully informed her great-niece about.

Allura felt as though her emotions were on a roller-coaster. She had no idea what to do and felt as alone as when her parents died all those years ago.

One day, while she was checking her e-mails, Allura was astonished to see that Bassel had written, saying that he was coming to Egypt for a visit. She eagerly wrote back, and her spirits instantly lifted.

Allura spent the next few days with her aunt, discussing her situation in depth, as she recovered. When the doctors gave her a clean bill of health, Nahed was right by her side when she petitioned the court for a divorce. Allura had decided she wanted nothing to do with Ahmed anymore.

Twenty Years Later

Chapter 25

Light at the End of the Tunnel

"Daddy, my line is getting heavy. I think I caught a big fish! Come check it out!"

"Yes, it is a big fish! Nice work, Sara! Come, help me pull the rod," said Bassel, who was spending time fishing with his fourteen-year-old daughter by the bay at their beach resort.

It had been nearly twenty years since Allura's troubled marriage to Ahmed and subsequent divorce. Their breakup had taken its toll on her, but that didn't stop her from completing her master's degree in journalism and mass communications. She and Bassel had entered into a three-year courtship, which ended in a union blessed by her aunt.

Shortly after he returned to Egypt, the two felt a spark returning. It was as if her life was starting all over again, and she couldn't wait to see what else was in store for her.

A year after Bassel and Allura got married, they had a baby girl, Sawsan, named after Allura's mother. Two years later, Sara came along.

Allura seized every opportunity she got to reunite with her father's family, whom she eventually introduced to Bassel and her two girls. They grew close and frequently gathered in each other's houses.

Now, they were celebrating their seventeenth wedding anniversary at their favourite beach resort. While Bassel and Sara were fishing, Allura and Sawsan were inside the house preparing a special lunch. Looking out of the kitchen window that overlooked the bay, Allura began to tear up as she watched her husband and youngest daughter bond.

"Mum, what's wrong?" asked Sawsan, who noticed her mum getting emotional.

"Oh, Sawsan, if only you knew how much you, your sister and your father mean to me, you would ache. Your heart would hurt."

"Then why the tears, Mum? Why are you crying?"

"These are tears of happiness, honey. I'm just a bit emotional. I'm proud of you and your sister, and for some reason I just remembered my parents again. It's not like I ever forget them, but there are moments when I feel them here, just here, right beside me. I was about your age when they passed away. Did I ever tell you that?"

Sawsan shook her head.

"How I wish they could have lived long enough to see us as a family and to meet you and your sister – especially you, Sawsan. I named you Sawsan for a reason. From the second I laid eyes on you, I could just see my own mother. You're a spitting image of her. The moment you opened your little eyes and blinked at the lights in the operating room, I saw a clear image of Mum. You're a blessing, you and your sister both. You're my world."

"Thanks, Mum. That's an honour. I wish I could have met Grandma too. She seemed to be an amazing person. Then again, so are you, Mum. You're about the strongest woman I know, not because you're Mum, but because you truly are very special."

Sawsan had two more years to go before graduating from school. Like her parents, she was a fantastic swimmer. But similar to Allura when she was younger, she wasn't sure if it was something that she wanted to pursue fully, despite Bassel's best attempts to convince her otherwise.

The couple had decided to open a business together shortly after their marriage. They turned Nahed's home, which she had left to Allura, into a centre for children with special needs. Bassel helped with sports and recreational activities including swimming, and Allura managed the marketing and logistics at the centre. They employed some of the best doctors, educators and specialists in Egypt, and became one of the most reputable special needs centres in the country, while offering the children one of the most reputable educational curriculums, tailor-made for children with special needs.

Both Bassel and Allura travelled frequently, with the girls alongside whenever possible, to attend workshops, trainings and sessions about some of the best practices for children with special needs. The centre's standards were benchmarked against some of the world's top special education programmes and quickly grew popular, with many trusting families enrolling their children there. The waiting list was long. Allura was adamant about fitting in all the children who needed that type of care, so she and Bassel were working on opening another location nearby.

Unlike her first marriage, Allura's second one was firmly built on a foundation of love, trust and mutual respect. She was grateful that God had blessed her with two beautiful young girls and a loving, understanding husband like Bassel, especially after her miscarriage and subsequent divorce. Her experience with Ahmed left her lost and lonely, but the minute she met Bassel after so many years apart, it occurred to both of them that they'd actually belonged together from the very beginning. They had been high school sweethearts and remained the best of friends, despite the distance.

A few years later after they got married, Nahed moved to Canada, claiming that it was time for her to reconnect with her son and his family. Allura stayed in constant touch with her despite the distance.

"Mum, can I ask you something? Do you and Dad still love each other the same way you did when you first met?" asked Sawsan as they were setting the dining table, which was perfectly located at their sea-view patio.

Allura smiled.

"Sawsan, I met your father when I was about seventeen years old. We had known each other since high school. Even though he moved away, we always stayed in touch. Despite the distance, he helped me a lot, especially during some very dark moments in my life. When he came back to Egypt for a visit, we reconnected straight away and have been inseparable ever since."

"Wow, Mum, that's so romantic. I wish I could feel that way for someone someday."

"That all depends on you. See, Sawsan, one thing I've learnt is that life's all about choices. It's the type of choice you make that structures the way for you. So if you want to be happy, make sure you end up with someone who'll make you happy. And if he doesn't make you happy, just leave. It's as simple as that."

"But how can you tell whether that person is the right one? I mean, you yourself got married before meeting Dad and thought he was the right one, but it turned out the opposite of what you had expected!"

"Well, from my experience I can say that the most important factors to consider are respect and upbringing. You need to make sure that the guy you are about to get involved with is respectful with you, his family, his friends and all types of people regardless of their status. As Grandma Nahed always said, 'We Egyptians are expected to take part in various familial duties and obligations once married.' So you need to remember that you're marrying his family as well as him. That was a problem with my first husband, but your father's family has always been wonderful with me."

"That sounds complicated, Mum. I hope my future husband will have a nice family too."

"Well, sometimes you might get stuck with in-laws that aren't the most pleasant to be around, but if you both truly love each other, you'll find a compromise that suits everyone. And if you don't, then it's up to you to decide whether to leave or stay."

Just then, Bassel and Sara walked into the kitchen with a cool box full of freshly caught fish.

"Look what we brought for you two beautiful ladies! Fish, fish and more fish!" said Bassel with a cheerful grin on his face as he placed a soft kiss on Allura's lips while placing the box on the kitchen counter.

"Not on my kitchen counter, please! I don't want it to smell like fish!" said Allura.

"Sorry about that. I'll just take them outside where the sun will melt the ice. At least that'll save you from having to defrost them when it's time to cook."

"No, no, don't do that! They'll rot!" answered Allura with a mock frown on her face as her family laughed. "Let's take a look at this magic haul of yours and choose which one we'll have for dinner," she said, opening the cool box. "Oh my, that's a whole lot of fish! While Sawsan and I scale them, you and Sara take a shower; you're stinking up the entire house!"

"Yes, commander!" Bassel said with a mock salute before ushering his daughter out.

While they were freshening up, Allura and Sawsan cleaned the fish and began preparing the barbecue on the patio.

"Mum! Look!"

Allura turned towards her daughter, spying the gut-covered object in her hands.

"Ewww! What is that, Sawsan? That looks repulsive! Throw it away!"

"I think it's a box or something! Let's clean it up and see!"

"A box? Ummm, fine. Bring it over to the sink."

A few seconds later, a small wooden box appeared in the palm of Sawsan's hand.

"What is it, Mum? Can I open it?"

Allura looked at it curiously, an idea emerging in her mind.

"Sure, let's see what treasure of the deep your father and sister caught."

Opening the box, they gasped at what laid within. A beautiful sapphire and diamond ring was nestled in the soft, satin material.

"Oh wow, Mum, that's gorgeous! It looks too big for me. Try it on!"

Just then, Bassel entered the room.

"I see you've uncovered our treasure. Here, let's see if it fits."

In a smooth gesture, he slipped it onto Allura's finger before gently kissing her hand. Looking into her eyes, he gently said: "It's perfect."

Allura blushed, letting out a wet giggle as she wiped away tears.

"Hey now, no tears. This is a happy occasion! Come, let's celebrate!" suggested Bassel as the family headed outside.

They all enjoyed a great meal on the patio overlooking the mesmerising blue sea. The sun was setting, and the view was breath taking. Everyone was relaxed and happy.

As the pleasant meal wound down, Bassel brought Allura's hand up for another kiss.

He found it the perfect opportunity to express himself.

"Allura my love, many people these days feel that their marriage is monotonous. That warm fuzzy feeling that once made you all tingly inside vanishes before you know it, those sweaty palms that get you all excited the second you both touch, eventually becomes a memory, and what once felt like love turns into convenience."

"Here we go again," said Sawsan, rolling her eyes with a playful smile.

Ignoring his eldest daughter's comment, Bassel went on. "To me, you have always been alluring, everything about you, your smile, your laugh, your face, the way you speak, who you are…you are powerfully and mysteriously attractive and fascinating; seducing, just like your name suggests! I still have sweaty palms around you…and…well…that tingling feeling…I still get it. You will never understand how much you mean to me, because there is no amount of words that can begin to describe my feelings for you."

"Too much information, Dad," interrupted Sawsan, with a sneaky grin.

Bassel got down on his knees to where Allura was seated.

"Allura, my precious, beloved partner, my wife and mother to my kids, my gorgeous woman, I just want you and our two beautiful girls to know that on this day seventeen years ago, I was the happiest man on earth, and I still am. You are about the purest women I've ever met. Happy anniversary, my love, and many more to come."

Allura got down on her knees to where Bassel was kneeling and hugged her loyal partner. She stretched both her arms, reaching out for her two girls. Hugging Bassel, Sawsan and Sara all at once, felt like she owned the world. Her life finally felt complete.

Looking up, she thanked God for everything she had accomplished. Bassel and her kids made up for all the tough times she had been through. She was on a mission to keep her chin up, stay positive and maintain the loving relationship she had always shared with her family.

She knew Sawsan and Haitham would never stop looking out for her. Whenever things got tough, she kept going back to her personal diary, where she had written some of her favourite quotations. One in particular came to mind just then: 'Hardships often prepare ordinary people for an extraordinary destiny.'

Allura realised that nobody had the right to underestimate her. While she was not perfect, she was a woman of ethics who simply wanted to be happy. The minute she was understood, her life started to make complete sense. It was the perfect end to a long and bumpy road, one that she wouldn't change for anything in the world.

The End